Type

"S"uperWoman

Type

"S"uperWoman

Finding the LIFE in Work-Life Balance: A Self-Searching Book for Women

Dr. Jaime Kulaga, Ph.D, LMHC

Dedication

I dedicate this book to women who are trying to balance their plates to keep those around them happy and content.

To those women who have found the courage to walk away in tough situations and for those who have the courage to stay in tough situations. To the women who put smiles on their faces, shake their heads "yes," even though their minds say "no," and then go into the bathroom to cry. I dedicate this to you.

It is my hope that this book will provide women seeking Life fulfillment with the tools necessary to help them control their own lives, make better decisions and find happiness.

CONTENTS

INTRODUCTION

CHAPTER 1

Life Roles 6

CHAPTER 2

Confidence, Disguised Aggression 22

CHAPTER 3

Defining your Barriers 33

CHAPTER 4

Uncomfortable is Most Comfortable 52

CHAPTER 5

Success Tracking 66

CHAPTER 6

Defining your Goals 81

CHAPTER 7

It's Not Only Okay to Ask for Help, It's Mandatory 95

CHAPTER 8

Your Story 105

CHAPTER 9

Type "S"uperWoman 114

CERTIFICATE

SuperWoman Certificate 131

Introduction

Work is more than your 9-5 job or career that pays the bills. Children are work, staying in shape is work, housework is work, caregiving is work, dating is work, being a spouse is WORK! If all of these things are work, then you might step back and realize that you do not have much of a Work-Life balance. The problem is, women barely have enough time to be workers, lovers, moms, bill payers, grocery shoppers, exercisers, schedulers, chauffeurs, caregivers, teachers and learners seven days per week, that there is no way we could actually have a Life, right? We often feel that we can't. We then rationalize that lover, mom, bill payer, grocery shopper, exerciser, scheduler, chauffeur, caregiver, teacher and learner are Life and not Work. We then join the rest of the people on the Ferris Wheel of non-fulfillment. We will literally spend our lives circling around the same things every day, forgetting that our "life" is not our "Life."

I began touring southern Florida with the Superwomen workshops mid-2013. I had a full coaching clientele, primarily made up of women. Several of the women would ask me to help them locate women's groups or workshops. I would search for workshops and couldn't really find one that would give the women an experience that they would not forget, yet best suit what they both wanted and needed. As I searched for various types of workshops, I found some that were about 45 minutes in length touching on the basics of Work-Life balance and fulfillment. My clients knew the basics, they

1

needed something more advanced. Then, I found advanced workshops that lasted a week for thousands of dollars in California or Texas. These workshops were impractical for the women that I was working with. Going away and leaving jobs and families was a bit, too, advanced. I felt like Goldilocks and the three bears. This one was too little, this one was too much, but nothing was "just right."

One day, while sitting at my desk, out of nowhere I got this fabulous idea. Why don't I lead a workshop specifically for women? I have the experience directly with women, I have completed research on women, and my clients are asking me for this; took a $300,000 Ph.D. to figure this one out! That is when I began creating the SuperWoman workshop. This book carries a lot of the concepts and content discussed within the workshops. The workshops have empowered women and helped women to reach goals, take responsibility for their lives and utilize tools to better their personal stories. I decided that writing this book would allow women all over the country to take part in this SuperWoman series. It is in this book that you will learn to become a SuperWoman. Soon you will find out that a Super Woman (two words) should not be mistaken for a SuperWoman (one word).

Women are smart and we have most of the answers, the right answers, sorry guys. We sacrifice one more day of our sanity because "our day is coming." We are the gender that skips using the bathroom when we have to go, just to get one more thing done. We know that if we keep pushing, success and personal fulfillment will come. This statement is very much true, to an extent. The problem is, once a woman reaches what she deems as successful, she is already in this habit of giving up herself to something else or putting someone else's needs first. This habit keeps us on the Ferris Wheel of non-fulfillment. When our chance comes to step off the ride, we unconsciously, or sometimes even consciously, decide to give the carnival boy another ticket to ride again.

Have you ever completed your day early, finished a project or are waiting on something to come through and you find yourself with just a few hours of a break, and then you panic? You literally create unnecessary extra work for yourself. God forbid you actually just sit there and enjoy the moment. This is the addiction of Work, and perhaps the feeling of guilt at its finest. Guilt tends to stop women from doing things for themselves. Successful and fulfilled people do take breaks. Real SuperWomen do take breaks. Aren't the most successful and fulfilled people the ones who say, "Work hard, Play hard?"

In my SuperWoman workshops, all the women are provided with journals. During the course of the workshop the women are advised to take notes on things they liked, emotions that arose, or statements that may have triggered thoughts, ideas or emotions. The women are to take notes of questions they have or anything that might come to mind that they deem of importance during the four hour event. I want you to take part in this experience, too. Grab a journal or notebook. As you read this book, you are going to question aspects of yourself, certain emotions might arise, or you may write down long lost ideas, passions or concerns you once had. Whatever comes to your mind that you deem is important, write it out. Also, I provide examples on marriage, dating, children, and employment throughout this book. If a specific example that I have referenced in a section does not pertain to you, that does not necessarily mean that all of the processes, consequences or techniques provided should be dismissed. Try to take each example and apply it to other areas of your life. Lastly, feel free to take notes within the context of this book.

Holding in your thoughts and ideas as we search for your fulfillment and desires puts you right back where you are now, the starting line. You have all these ideas, goals and dreams in your head. Every day, the day to day agenda forces you to push all those goals back into a file in your mind, because you "don't have time for that." Now the file is lost, and together we are going to recover it. The more you take notes in this book, are interactive during activities and use your journal, the more fulfillment you will find. Even after reading this book, I recommend maintaining a journal. Write in your journal at least three times per week. Not only does journaling help to let out built up emotions from the day, but it also helps you to think before you act. Be cautious of impulsive decision making. Write decisions that you are contemplating in your journal and go back to that entry in a day or two. Re-read what you wrote, does this still sound like a good idea? Journaling will also help you to note patterns of your behaviors. If you get anxious frequently, I encourage you to journal about when you feel anxious and the activities and thoughts leading up to those feelings. To note patterns of your behaviors it may take days or weeks to observe. Be patient. Finding fulfillment will be a process. This process is part of your journey, your story and your fulfillment.

This book is going to provide you with a variety of tips and exercises on how to create Work-Life balance. As a woman myself, I know that Work encompasses much more than "work" or, whatever pays the bills. A lot of things in life are Work and we cannot let these things become our only Life. There is more to the carnival than just the Ferris Wheel. Together we will also discover the definition of Life as it pertains to you, specifically. Work and Life are subjective to each woman. What might constitute as fulfillment to me might not be true fulfillment for you. Grab your capes future SuperWomen, as we are about to embark on a journey toward fulfillment and balance!

"Our main motivation for living is our will to find meaning in life."
-Viktor Frankl

Chapter 1

Life Roles

When I first began writing this book I was listening to the audio tape of *Lean In* by COO of Facebook, Sheryl Sandberg. A must read for women who want to be empowered, and empower other women. Sandberg really delves into the importance of women being aware of their status in society and how to overcome challenges in order to make women more equal. At one point early on in the book, Sandberg discussed how women do not want everything, they are afraid of losing everything. This statement made me think about women in general. How different would our lives or perspectives in decision making be if we did not fear losing something; losing likability, a lover, a friend, respect, our job, children, etc.?

In life coaching sessions with women clients, I rarely get an answer to the following question: "What do you like to do, just for you?" If the women do respond, here are typical responses: Yoga, massage, pedicure, nap. These activities are wonderful, but come on ladies, isn't there something else that we would like to do for us; something that would provide long term gratification and satisfaction? A manicure is not going to provide life fulfillment, it only provides immediate fulfillment. I am a mother, so I fully understand that we would pay someone $100 to let us nap for 15 minutes occasionally. However, what does that 15 minute nap do? It gives us immediate fulfillment, only to wake up and jump back on the Ferris Wheel faster and more quickly.

There are probably many things women would like to strive for or engage in, but we are conditioned to push harder for other things or other people. We are also very busy doing the things that "have" to get done, like cleaning the house and laundry. Those things that "have to get done" are part of the habit we have created for ourselves; it's our very own self-created Ferris Wheel. Using words like "have," "must," "should" and "ought" are words that fill us with guilt and anxiety. Women despise feeling guilty, thus to avoid feelings of guilt, we satisfy the "haves" in our lives before we satisfy ourselves. Women often do not deem themselves as a "have" or "must" in their own lives. When I tell women that they need to become a "have" in their own lives, a light bulb goes on in their heads, "oh, I guess I never thought of that."

Consistently satisfying the "have's" and "must's" as a priority becomes a potential threat to women's fulfillment. When I lead up the SuperWomen workshops, women are asked to take out a notecard and list out all of the life roles that they play. Women tend to list 20 or 30 life roles on an average. Life roles consist of the roles that the women play in their lives that consume their time and energy. Life roles can be anything from mother, wife, daughter, to laundry doer, friend's therapist, or dog walker. I have yet for a woman to put "me" on the list of their life roles. Laundry doer makes the list almost every time though. We have guilt for not doing the laundry or not satisfying a spouse, but we don't have guilt for not doing something for ourselves? This is a perfect recipe for lack of fulfillment and later life depression. If our personal perspective is that doing the laundry is something we "have" to do, and that we don't "have" to work on ourselves, we "have" a problem. When women do have time to focus on themselves, they have a sense of guilt for doing so. We have a double edge sword here. Were damned if we do work on ourselves (feelings of guilt for doing something for us) were damned if we don't work on us (then we lack long term Life fulfillment).

It is very important that women avoid using guilt and anxiety ridden words provoked by "have," "must," "should," and "ought." Eliminating these types of words will reduce feelings of guilt, even unconscious feelings of guilt we ignore or don't know about. Take a second to think about all the different phrases you say each day in which there is a "must," "should," "have" or "ought" attached to it. For example, "I really 'should' do X and Y." "I really 'should' 'have', X,Y." "Oh, I 'have' to X, Y." You are brainwashing yourself all day. You are literally planting seeds of guilt and anxiety into your own head hundreds of times per day. Doing anything in life hundreds of times per day is going to immediately put you in a habit of doing something a certain way. You are now in a habit of provoking your own guilt and anxiety. I want you to really focus on how many times each day you use these words. Work diligently to change the way you talk out loud and in your head. The only thing you "have" to do is breathe air. You "want" to do the laundry.

Believe it or not, laundry is a "want," not a "have." Change words of guilt into words of desire. "I 'want' to do X, Y." "I 'desire' to X,Y." This way, if we don't do the laundry or cook dinner for the night, our level of anxiousness or guilt will be decreased. Perhaps now you will have the energy to focus on something you "have" to do, like work on you. It is okay to skip cooking dinner a couple times a week to work-out, walk on the beach, or do something fulfilling. The only time you should use the word "have" is when you are talking about working on yourself, or if you are drowning and "have" to "have" air.

On our individual journey in finding out what Life is, we first need to learn about what might hold us back from trying to discover what we are truly passionate about, or what we want out of life. During my doctoral program, I completed research on women and abandonment. This was such an amazing experience for me because I got to delve into women's thought processes and emotions about abandonment and relationships in life. The ultimate in understanding experiences is a knowledge of the essences. The essence of a person is when they are broken down to their real nature. The results of my study had shown that fear was the one common underlying essence of the women's experiences in adult intimate relationships. This fear stemmed from repeated abandonment or fear of abandonment throughout their childhood and adult years.

F.E.A.R. False Evidence Appearing Real. Fear becomes a pattern and habit. Fear can become a way of life. Fear may be the underlying essence or barrier to fulfillment, but what do women fear? Research, as well as my personal experiences in working with women, has shown that many women fear feelings of guilt and loss. From early on in life, women internalize losses. Studies show that when fathers are absent from the home due to divorce or abandonment, girls are more likely to see that loss as something that is wrong with them. This is possibly the start of the fear of loss for some women, not to mention the self-esteem hit that must be taken with this type of internalization.

There is a quote by General Patton that says "Fear kills more people than death. Death kills us but once, but fear kills us over and over." This quote could pertain to a lot of different things, but for the purposes of this book, it pertains to our Life balance and fulfillment as women. If we fear the feeling of guilt behind doing something for ourselves or fear losing something or someone for venturing out to explore Life, we are not living Life. Every time we fear guilt or loss we are killing a dream we have for our Life. Eventually, this particular pattern of thought (desire something for our Life, let fear destroy idea, cease moving forward), becomes a pattern of self-destruction and self-sabotage.

As women begin creating families of their own, I have observed that they have less time to do the things that once provided them a sense of fulfillment. Logically, this makes sense to an extent. To add on something, we must cut back on other things. We add a life role, we drop a life role. But to lose oneself almost completely could create anger, depression or lack of fulfillment for that woman. Initially, most women enjoy giving themselves to their new lives. We enjoy making the husband happy and playing "wife." Then we have a baby and find ourselves overjoyed with all the new blessings. During this exciting time you might consciously give up things you like, but you do not mind because this is your family, and honestly, playing "house" is kind of fun. As time passes, you find yourself giving up more things that you like and making more sacrifices that you sometimes do not want to make. However, society is wonderful at making women feel guilty for choosing themselves over their families. How dare we?! It is at this very point that you have bought your first block of tickets for the Ferris Wheel ride. Life becomes consistent, structured, and cyclical. As you continue to pass up moments where you could do something for yourself, you then begin to cut off moments that could even lead up to identifying what you want. Before you know it, when asked what you like or what could provide fulfillment to you, you respond with, "I don't really know" or "yoga, massage, pedicure, nap."

Should we not tend to our families, should we put aside what "has" to get done in order to be selfish? Yes and no. Work and Life. Find your balance. It is not that we are trying to do something unethical or immoral, in which conscious guilt might actually be a good thing, but rather our very nature of caring and putting others first is hindering us to the point that we are spending our lives unfulfilled. Spouses, children and work are very important, but so are you. Pema Chödrön said, "Compassion for others begins with kindness to ourselves." You only get one life, that's it. People march on, and one day, even the children will, too.

The nature of a woman is based on care, nurturing, and being communal. In no way should women give up these characteristics. But here is the difference, Kindness ≠ Doormat. By nature, people are takers. You cannot fault people who take from you. If you are going to give and give and give, people are going to take and take and take. Set boundaries. Here is where the quote "Fool me once, shame on you. Fool me twice, shame on me" comes into play. As you get into a habit of giving and putting others first, you minimize yourself and forget what would even fulfill you. You begin to give, not even knowing why you are giving or how you got into this place. It is the habit, the structure and the cyclicality of your life that causes you to give again, almost unknowingly. Someone, please, halt the Ferris Wheel! Sometimes, we find ourselves in the middle of a panic attack just because we forgot X or Y on "our" to do list, and it is actually us taking on extra work for someone else. We are stealing other people's "to-do" lists and doing them. Stop stealing, it's illegal.

The average person takes on 15-25 life roles. Women find themselves reluctantly on the higher end. We like to be liked. When another life role is added onto our plate via child, husband, friend, family member or boss, we agree verbally, but scream "NO" on the inside. The problem is, people can't hear our thoughts, they take our word. Going back to the concept of fear, we wouldn't want our child, husband, friend, family member or boss to reject us, be upset with us, or not call upon us next time they have a task, so we opt to take on the next challenge, then go in the bathroom and cry.

Reality check, both women and men alike can typically only handle about five life roles. Take a strong look at all your life roles and evaluate only which top five are most important to you and your fulfillment in life. Once you can give time and attention to those areas in your life, you will be stronger in handling the less fulfilling or less demanding roles, like laundry doer and PTA mom. Let's say your top five life roles are: you, mother, wife, caregiver and employee. If you focus heavily on these areas you will not only feel better personally, but the respect and understanding that the people in these areas will give to you when you seek your own personal fulfillment will be heightened. You will need support in your journey of Life and fulfillment.

My Top Five Life Roles

1.ME_____

2._____

3._____

4._____

5._____

*For a printable version go to: www.typesuperwoman.com and click on the link that says, "SuperWoman Worksheets."

Strong and valuable support systems and people will be okay with you saying "no" to taking on certain tasks. Good supports, will tell you to say "no." As you say "no" you are setting boundaries with those you love and those you can't stand. If saying "no" is hard, practice saying "no" to those you feel safe with. Journal out some pre made responses to those who consistently ask you to take on additional roles you do not want to take on. Sometimes, as women, we have a very hard time saying "no" to men. Perhaps it goes back to the fear of loss. If you stand up to your male boss, you could lose your job. That is a real fear. Women are awesome at compromising. Use your very nature to your advantage. Try compromising with a boss regarding taking on an extra role. Women are communal. If you enjoy doing things as a team, try getting the family involved in a project you are taking on, or on the job, encourage coworkers to take part in what you are doing. Do not feel bad delegating out.

As I coach women, I sometimes feel that when I use the word delegate, I have cussed them out during the session. Some of the women look at me like the word must be foreign, while others think I have a devious plan to take control away from them. Women who have a tough time delegating out have gotten into a habit of taking on everything themselves. At a young age women create the foundation of this habit. As young adult women, we began to take on life roles left and right like we were super heroes. People commended us on our strength and abilities, and there were even some people that told us to "slow down." It was nice to be complimented and supported by the women who were older than us.

We had something to prove, we couldn't slow down. We had life planned out and what was ahead of us was exciting and "fulfilling." We could do it all. We skipped the journey and went right for the finish line.

After a while however, there were days that were exhausting and we wanted a break. The finish line was not the finish line. Were we tricked? The finish line was actually the beginning of another quest. We questioned ourselves, happiness and fulfillment. What we once would do that was considered kind by others now appears to be an expectation. Even you might expect that you should take on roles that are set in front of you despite your liking. Not only can you decline additional life roles, but you can actually delegate some of the responsibilities that are associated with your current life roles, out to others.

From my experiences in working with older women, I have found that the concept of delegating is sometimes non-existent. Sixty years ago, times were much different than they are now. A lot more women worked from home. Many women were married by 21 years of age and their profession was motherhood. Presently, to maintain a household, many families need two incomes. Older women have adapted to the changing times and got a career outside of the home, but never let go of some of the responsibilities from their job within the home. They added a role and didn't drop a role. The issue here is that women have taken on a second full time job (Job 1, in home, Job 2, outside of home). Working 80 hours or more per week, plus all the stress that comes from having two jobs leads to a decrease in Life fulfillment and an increased chance of depression. Research shows that women are three times more likely than men to attempt suicide. Women tend to use "beautifying" manners to attempt suicide, such as taking pills. Men tend to use more destructive manners to kill themselves, such as using a gun. Chances of death are higher when a more lethal method is used. This is the reason that more men die when they attempt suicide compared to women. What is important to note though, is that more women than men attempt suicide. Depression and leading an unfulfilled life play a role in these women's suicide attempts. Sadly, the cohort of women aged 60-64 has seen the largest jump in suicide rates. This rate has jumped almost 60% since 1999.

One of my aunts is in her sixties. She came from a strong Italian background. She shares stories of helping my nana cook in the kitchen when she was younger. One of the responsibilities of cooking was serving the man first. When dinner was done, my aunt and nana would serve my papa first, then the two brothers. Once the men were served, then my aunt and nana would serve themselves. I have noticed this pattern continue throughout the years. When I was younger and would go to my nana's house, my papa and father would always be served first.

In my world now, when I am cooking, I serve my children first to get them to calm down and then pass out the rest of the food, sit and eat. Running two businesses together, my husband and I are forced to be a team. We cook the food together, and get it on the table together. We high five at the end of the meal just at the shear fact that we got through another chore and the children are still alive! It is funny how times have changed.

I recently visited my aunt and her hospitality was wonderful. However, I noticed that her habit of putting others first and then herself, still remains. My aunt's friend came over and she created a beautiful meal for all of us. We were all outside in the pool enjoying the moment and I noticed that she was inside cooking. She indicated that she liked to cook and that it would not take her long. She missed "the moment." The issue is that her selflessness and habit of putting others first has literally caused her to miss moments in life that may lead to her feeling more fulfilled.

Women in their 60's have been shaped by stories of strength and resilience. Many women in this cohort have faced divorces, loss of a spouse or health issues. These life changing events instill a need for Life fulfillment. Women in their 20's do not desire Life fulfillment the way that women in their 40's, 50's, 60's and 70's desire it. At age 60, just starting to find fulfillment out of life can be scary. Searching for yourself at any point in life is scary, but as we age, we have other factors that can interrupt the self-searching process, such as health concerns.

Whether you are an adolescent or in later life adulthood, pausing to reflect on the moment is essential. My aunt genuinely loves cooking, I believe that. However, it is also important to look at what is happening in the moment and weigh where your attention should be. If you invite people over to spend time with them, give them your time. I notice similar interactions with family, friends and clients during the holiday season. They spend all their time prepping, stressing, cooking, serving and cleaning up, that not only did they miss the moment of the holiday season, but they are glad it is over. This holiday season, set boundaries and limit yourself to what you can handle emotionally. Be sure that you enjoy the holiday, too. Remember who your top five life roles consist of, and don't go overboard serving all the people outside of those roles. Typically, as you stress about serving others for the holidays, you complain to the ones you actually care most about. You do not want your joy of pleasing others to become something that people now expect all the time from you. Kindness $\neq$ Doormat.

When you are in a moment, ask yourself the following questions: What about this moment do I enjoy? If I am not enjoying this moment, why not? Are my priorities where they should be? Could I delegate out some of what I am doing to someone else?

Here is a perfect example of taking on extra roles and not delegating. As I was promoting a new business venture, I decided to join a networking group. This group was a weekly commitment and required me to meet one on one with several people each week in addition to the weekly meeting. There were commitments to being in the group, and I knew this up front. I kept rationalizing these responsibilities with the fact that successful people work hard, and this was part of what I "had" to do. About one month into the group I was asked to take on a leadership role. There was no pay for this role and I was to put in more time and commitment, both of which I did not have.

When I was asked to take over the leadership role, I was grateful for the opportunity and did not want to disappoint the group. I also feared (again with the fear concept), that saying "No" to this opportunity would make me not look like the super woman everyone thought I was. Here is Jaime, the one who keeps adding to her plate, and yet still shines and doesn't fail. Little did these people know, things were failing, and I was tired. Worse, my top five life roles were not being satisfied and I felt a lot of guilt about that. I let fear take precedence, and while my brain scram, "Hell NO! Are you kidding?!" to the gentleman asking me to take on this role, my voice said "Yes, I would love this opportunity." I immediately called my husband and told him what I did. Not only did he think I was insane and told me to take back my "yes," but looking back, I must have caused him disappointment. He is my top life role. At this point in my life, I wasn't fulfilling him and giving my time to him. Now, the little time I did have, I was going to give it to a networking group. That was not a responsible choice. I did more harm than good to everyone, even myself, just by trying to avoid the guilt of saying "no" and the fear associated with possibly not being offered a leadership role in the future.

Women work really hard to be credible and gain authority. The one thing you do not want to do as a woman is say "yes" to something and then take your word back. This is exactly what I did with this networking group. After one month into the role, I began slipping on my commitments. I was not carrying my fair weight in group exercises and I was embarrassed. I consequently emailed an apology letter to my teammates and resigned from my position. Not only did I say "yes" and then turn around and say "no," I emailed them that I dropped out. How impersonal! I felt as if I lost credibility, and I probably did. I did not mean to fail them. I appreciated everything they did for me and liked these people as professionals and some as friends. It was my personal inability to know and understand my boundaries that I did not meet expectations. I have learned the importance of speaking up since this event. If I would have acknowledged the position, been grateful and politely declined, they would have probably respected me more. More opportunities come up. If we reframe and begin to see things in a different light, we probably will have an influx of opportunities that would come up each day for us. This networking group is wonderful, but based upon who I am and what life roles are important to me, this was something I should have not considered at that specific time in my life. I was unable to drop a role to add this one and I learned a lesson from it.

I was recently asked to present at an upcoming International Learning Seminar. My topic is on Humor in the Courseroom and falls along the lines of my teaching position at a University. The preparation for this presentation is going to take my time and energy in order for this to be a success. I have a lot of prep work both physically and mentally for this presentation. From my experiences with the networking group, I have grown. I understand my responsibilities and life roles. I want to do everything, but I can't, that's the reality. Thus, I evaluated my top five life roles prior to agreeing to present at the learning seminar. I examined which life roles I couldn't change or did not want to change. Then I made the decision that I will stop the SuperWomen workshops for a couple months so I can channel my energy into the new presentation. When that presentation is completed, I can then drop that role and add SuperWoman workshop back onto my plate. In order to be effective, I have dropped a role to add one. Women can do anything they want, but they can't do everything.

Take time to reflect on some of the following questions: What have you taken on in the past that you should not have taken on? Why did you take this on? Did you lose credibility? What was the biggest lesson for personal growth that you learned from this experience? What is currently on your plate that you can delegate out?

"Sometimes you have to forget what you "have" to do, to remember what you deserve." -Unknown

Chapter 2

Confidence, Disguised Aggression

Girls grow up being showered in pink and boys, in blue. From before birth, children are pushed a certain direction unknowingly and sometimes unwelcomingly. The psychology of the color blue is that it represents reliability and responsibility. The color blue reflects inner security and self-confidence. Blue stands for having direction in life. Pink, on the other hand, represents nurturing, love and compassion. Pink reduces feelings of aggression. Research suggests that large amounts of the color pink can literally create a physical weakness in people. Girls grow to want dolls and wedding dresses, a sign of nurturing and compassion. Boys engage in backyard football and gun fights. This enhances skills like being aggressive and competitive.

Whenever I am asked to speak on the topic of Work-Life Balance to women, there is always one portion of the seminar in which I go around and ask several of the women the following question: "What is the best advice you have ever been given?" Go ahead. Take a moment and answer this for yourself. During the workshops, the women give answers such as, "Never give up," "Find your passion," "Treat others as you want to be treated," or "Do what makes you happy." There are endless quotes, and some really great ones for that matter that these women have provided to me. When I was sitting in a seminar in which a man was leading up, a similar question was asked to the audience. The first man who responded to the question, his words stuck with me. He said "The best advice I was ever given was given to me by my father when I was a young boy. He told me I must be *aggressive* in life, work and love." This was such a wakeup call for me. This man was taught from early in life to be aggressive in everything he does. Women are told to "push hard" and "never give up" but words like "be aggressive," are rarely ever told to us. Think about this word and what it really means for a second. Aggressive? Not the word "tough," not "strong," but, aggressive. Aggressive is almost bully like, especially if a woman is aggressive. If the theories regarding the color pink hold true, and pink does reduce aggression, are women doomed from the start? On the other hand, do I, as a woman, personally really want to be known as being aggressive in a society that probably is not going to change overnight? Not really. But I do think women need to be more aggressive with their desires and goals.

The sad reality is that after writing this book, there still will be discrimination against women. Women still will be called "a bitch" for being overly aggressive and might even lose promotions for seemingly being too pushy or, not a "team player." Honestly, I do think women need to be cautious in how aggressive they are because it could backfire on them. I wish it didn't, but society isn't going to change tomorrow. Changing society is a work in progress. We can be a part of this progressive change, but chances are, change won't be tomorrow. The good news is, women have the tools and skills that can make us triple aggressive in an incognito way if we just become more self-aware. Being aggressive like a man does not have to be the same type of aggressive for a woman. An "aggressive" woman might be able to make demands, be successful and get what she wants by showing confidence and standing up for herself using the appropriate language. Being fulfilled in life and stepping off of the Ferris Wheel makes you stronger and more confident. Confidence is a form of aggression. Many women lack confidence. Women are most critical of themselves. Women also tend to have high levels of self-doubt. Your math word problem of the day: Aggression to a man is like confidence to a woman.

When applying to a new job, a woman can use confidence as her form of aggression. For instance, let's say that you have a job interview for a promotional position within a company. Go into the interview knowing that you are going to get the job. You are not going to Jinx the job if you go in confident! You are actually jinxing the job if you go in not being confident. Some women pre-game their interview with a lack of confidence by saying, "I hope I get this job" or "I really need this job." Start out by saying "I have worked my ass off for this position, it is mine!" If you are needy, you're not going to get this advancement, if you are confident, you will. Do not compare yourself to the guy who is the boss's favorite or the woman who has more experience than you. Maybe they will get the position over you, but if you go in with that mind-set from the start your brain will try to prove itself right.

I always tell my clients, do not live the same pain twice, especially if the pain might be unnecessary. If you create anxiety and tell yourself, "I won't get the job" and then you in fact don't get the job, then you lived the pain twice. Once before you didn't know if you got the job or not and once after you really didn't get the job. If you tell yourself, "I won't get the job," and then you do get the job, you lived the pain initially for no reason. This goes for everything in life. Do not stress out until it's time to stress.

Take a moment to think about different times in your life in which you have worried unnecessarily or when you worried before the event even took place. Now, think about how many times the event went smooth and nothing negative happened. Everything was fine, or better than fine in the end. How much unnecessary energy did you spend worrying? What else could you have done for you or your fulfillment in place of that worrying?

Look at some of the choices you have made in life. Take time to reflect on your successes and what you have done right. Do not just think about your successes, write them out, at least ten. Then, take the time to reflect on those successes and your choices and try to remember how you felt. The reason it is important to highlight your successes and the good choices that you make on a daily basis, is to help increase your confidence. As women, we are really good at seeing the good in others, but the bad in ourselves. If we mess up or are not right, we are very critical with ourselves. The reduction in confidence is depleted much more quickly than when we do something right and should have an increase in confidence. When you are aware of your pattern of good choices, when you make bigger decisions or interact with authorities, you come across more confident. Confidence is the female form of male aggression. If you behave and talk in an interview with confidence, you instantly give off a vibe that you are strong, powerful and the "right" type of aggressive.

Women can also use confidence when up against the "aggressive male." I have found that when women are most vulnerable in life, they are often placed in front of a man. For example, in situations of divorce, loss of a job, or death of a loved one, we might find ourselves seeking out an attorney, accountant, or law enforcement. These are male dominated fields. When a woman has to make a major life changing decision, there is a high likelihood that at some point she will be guided by a man in some respects. It is important that even in the most challenging of times, you call upon your confidence. In low points of our lives, even if we caused them, you need to reflect on the good decisions that you have made in the past. Create a list of your successes when you are strong and on a good path. When you become vulnerable or tired, take out this sheet to reflect upon your good choices.

When we present ourselves as vulnerable or emotional, people will sweep in and guide us in the direction that they think is best, without even really knowing what we need or want. All people have motives. People might not want to hurt you deliberately, but the fact is, only you live your life and walk in your shoes. No one really knows what is best for you, except you. If someone makes a decision on your behalf, and it's the wrong choice, they march on, and you are stuck figuring the rest out. In a vulnerable state, bring your confidence to the table. If you feel that you are being pressured or your gut is telling you that something is not right, you can say "no," get a second opinion, or tell people you need to reflect on the situation and will come back to it.

I always tell my clients, "no impulsive decisions!" This goes for breaking up with boyfriends, leaving a job, firing an employee, investing in stock, anything. When women make impulsive decisions, it is typically out of emotion. Think about being at the Supermarket. Supermarkets have those little end caps right at check out with the mascaras, magazines, gums and sodas. When you are in line and quickly grab a magazine, it is a last minute impulsive purchase. It is not really what you wanted from the Supermarket, but, based out of instant gratification and impulsivity, you grabbed the item. When you go home, if you regret buying the magazine, it is really not the end of the world, it was four bucks. However, if you impulsively break up with a loved one, that is going to cost you more than a magazine. Making the decision to break up was not really what you wanted, but you did it based out of instant gratification of getting the last word or proving a point.

In coaching sessions, my clients that often make impulsive decisions take part in a painting activity. When people break up a relationship impulsively, they often say hurtful things that they do not mean. During the painting activity, clients are asked to place ink blots of various colors onto white computer paper. Each ink blot is spread around and the individual colors represent a time that they said or did something to someone that was hurtful. Once they have completed this task, I politely ask them to take a rag and erase all the blots of paint and bring the piece of paper back to white. Needless to say, this can't be done. The point of the activity is that when you say or do something to hurt someone, even if you take back your words and apologize, you have scarred them. Impulsivity scars. It scars partners, you and entire relationships.

Making impulsive decisions decreases our confidence because those decisions are not strong and had little thought behind them. Even worse, if you end a relationship abruptly, and really don't want to, as you beg for the person back, you use time and energy. You also forfeit some of your personal control and have ruined your credibility within the relationship; clearly, not a confidence boosting process. The more impulsive decisions you make, the more you will find that your decision making process is not very good. Repeated patterns of poor decision making, decreases a woman's confidence. To increase your confidence, take more time to reflect on situations before making a decision. Reflection takes more than 20 minutes. Reflection can take days, weeks or even months of journaling and talking to support systems to come to a rational, clear headed, open minded decision. Get in a habit of processing decisions in this manner. This way, when you are in a vulnerable state or are confronted with someone stronger, you will have a habit of listening to them and taking your own space and time to reflect before coming to a conclusion.

Raising children is another area within life that mothers need to be confident. In therapy, I have worked with mothers who feel responsible for all the wrong their children do. I previously worked with a mother who had an adolescent daughter that was acting out. Her daughter was acting up in school and she thought it was because of a divorce years back. My client had been abused verbally and physically, and she still says that if she just would have "stuck it out" for her daughter, her daughter wouldn't be having "all this trouble" in school.

As much as I value marriage and think that couple's should work through problems, abuse is something that should not be tolerated. Just as children only get one life, so do you. It is not selfish to walk away from abuse. Of course, there is much more to walking away, than actually, walking away. There are real fears and the need for supports and protection that come along with this process. Walking away from any relationship that is hurtful to you takes confidence and courage. There is a reason many women stay in abusive relationships. It is not easy to pick up and begin again. Women face another double edged sword. She feels damned if she stays, and initially feels damned if she leaves.

If you are a woman that does walk away from abuse, you should reward yourself. In the situation with my client, maybe divorce does play a role in the daughter acting out, but it is not fair, nor is it reality, to say that the divorce is the only reason for her behavior. Adolescents are well aware of the choices they make. They are also influenced by other extraneous variables like peers, the educational system, hormones, and just trying to find their own identity in general. Since there are so many other variables that could be playing a role in this adolescent's behavior, the mother should not place blame solely onto one source, herself. Even if we could somehow identify that 100% of the daughter's acting out was solely because of the mother, then I suppose we would find that we have an imperfect mother. Not perfect? Yes! Ladies, we are not perfect. All of us have imperfections. Thinking that you have to be perfect at anything in life is not only a barrier to your goals and Life fulfillment, but you have directly set yourself up for failure. Nothing and no one is perfect. You will not be the first person on earth to be perfect. Don't spend your life trying to be something that doesn't exist. One of my favorite quotes was said by Thomas Edison, "I failed my way to success."

The way women communicate is also really important in demonstrating confidence. Communicate with confidence to get the results you desire; these results lead to Life fulfillment. Sometimes our forms of communication can discredit, sexualize or embarrass us. The way that men talk and communicate is not how women should talk and communicate. Women are different and society sees us as being different. No, it is not fair that Tom can be confrontational with the boss and somehow consequently be promoted, whereas in the same situation you will be fired or ridiculed, but life is not fair. Be that incognito aggressive we discussed earlier. Instead of being confrontational, use your strengths in determination and being communal to move yourself forward. Be confident. If you want something from your boss, take time to scope out what type of personality he has. When was your boss most receptive to you? Why was he receptive? What did your non-verbal communication, communicate? If you can prep for a situation, you have set yourself up for success. In preparation for asking for something, analyze who you think will be at your meeting, know ahead of time what your objective is, and prepare how to respond to critical comments so that you are not cornered. Do not walk into situations leading with emotion. Being overly excited, anxious, sad or downright angry can create a negative situation for you and even deplete some of your hard earned credibility. Also, never let someone else put you down in order to raise themselves up. Speak up with confidence to protect yourself. Speaking up with confidence is different from speaking up with emotion. Use that incognito aggression so that you maintain your credibility and the accomplishments you have created are noticed.

I have learned that as a woman, when you communicate with people, you should not start out with "I think" or "I feel," especially in business. This was very challenging for me work on initially, and still is something I need to be cognizant of when I speak. The rationale is that business is business and we should keep out our feelings and emotions. However, I think, (I suppose that is contradictory) that as women, we should apply the no "I think, I feel" rule to our personal lives, too. Here is my theory. Many women discredit themselves, have low self-esteem and self-confidence and frequently doubt themselves. If a woman who frequently doubts herself says, "I think I should write a book," then she has placed doubt in the very context of her Life goal. If she already doubts herself in general, than anything she "thinks" she would like to do, could be wrong. She is much more likely to succumb to riding the Ferris Wheel when she couples her guilt about putting herself first with added self-doubt. If you really want to write a book, say, "I will write a book." I now have backed up my Life goal with confidence and determination, a couple of incognito aggressive womanly characteristics.

Women are not perfect, we do have to ask for help along the way and we are different from men. As a woman, we can use our confidence and language to be successful and find fulfillment. If you are finding that your Work-Life balance consists of primarily of Work, then it is time that you become a bit more aggressive, I mean confident, in Life.

"No one can make you feel inferior without your consent."- Eleanor Roosevelt

Chapter 3

Define your Barriers

Before we move on to exploring what you desire in Life, you first need to know what is stopping you from pursuing your Life. Awareness of the self and barriers is essential in helping women grow and find Life balance. When you tell yourself you "can't" do something because X, Y, or Z you stop your brain from forward thinking. You ride the Ferris Wheel, again. Even if you could find a way to do something for your Life, the word "can't" stops the brain from even trying to find a solution. If it "can't" be done, why even waste time trying?

Good people or things in your life can constitute as barriers as you move toward fulfillment. I love my children, to me, they are more important than any goal or life role. Many times, they are my goal. However, this does not mean that I have to set aside other desires that would help me achieve fulfillment. That is not selfish to say. My statement shows confidence in my ability to both raise my children effectively, and still have my own personal life fulfillment. Writing this book is a Life goal for me. I can love my children, take them to school, play with them, and still write a book. Maybe I will have to set aside some alone time for me and stay up late here and there to complete this book, but no one said this would be easy to do whether or not I had children. I am mother, wife, life coach, professor, speaker and now author? Am I nuts!? A little bit, but to keep my sanity and find fulfillment, I have to be nuts sometimes. I suppose I am being somewhat aggressive with my Life. I do not have to give my children up or my Life goals, just like you do not have to give up some of your "positive barriers" in order to find your fulfillment. Reframe your thinking. In regard to my example of children, there is no fear of loss here, just a win-win. I make sure that the time I am spending with my children is time that *they* see as valuable. In return, I get to work on my Life goals.

While completing research for my dissertation, I remember reading about bonding between a father and son versus a father and daughter. The example was that if a father spent three hours on the couch watching a football game with his son not saying one word, he might have bonded with his son. Whereas, if a father spent that same time on the same couch, but with his daughter, she may have sat there wondering the entire time if he was upset with her because he failed to talk with her. I want you to see that spending time with your children, *your* way, does not necessarily mean that is satisfying to *them*. Make sure all the moments you spend with the people in your top five life roles are spent efficiently and effectively. What do they perceive as valuable time with you? That's what you need to provide them with.

When you have set aside time for a life role, give it 100% of you. For example, if night times are for your children, then from 6pm-9pm make it about your children and not about work. Avoid answering calls, watching television or doing anything that the children would perceive as not spending time with them. If you have set aside time for a certain person, give your time to them. Who do you most fear losing in your life? Those are the people you want to give your most dedicated time to. When I satisfy my children's needs the way they perceive as satisfying, than they are more accepting of me working on my personal fulfillment. You can spend three hours with your child or partner, and if you are doing other things than focusing on them, this time can't be counted as time spent with them. Use your time efficiently and effectively. Instead of spending three hours with this person, spend one hour with them, but give them your undivided attention.

Another positive barrier as we work toward fulfillment could be our role as spouses or partners. The attention your partner perceives they are receiving is important in determining their satisfaction with their time spent with you. If you think just being at home is giving your spouse time, you are mistaken. I love the saying, "The grass isn't greener on the other side. It is greener where you water it." What does this mean to you and your current relationships? Just as children need to perceive you as spending time with them, so do your partners. If you have set a date night with your spouse or partner, be present with him. Avoid talking about work or children. Do things during that time alone with one another that you normally do not do in front of children, at work, or simply do not have time to do. There is a real importance in physical touch like kissing, holding hands and making love.

I suggest to couples in counseling to read *The Five Love Languages* by Gary Chapman. According to Chapman, we all have a primary love language: Quality Time, Physical Touch, Words of Affirmation, Receiving Gifts, Acts of Service. For instance, we may like special things said to us (words of affirmation), but do not really care too much about receiving gifts. The problem is, if our partner is doing things for us but is not satisfying our Primary Love language, then the marriage suffers. Knowing your partner's love language is not only important in keeping them happy, but it also important to know for times of disagreement.

A client of mine whose love language is words of affirmation recently got into an argument with her boyfriend whose love language is physical touch. While in the car arguing, he began to calm himself down and touched her arm. She was upset because he was not talking to her and telling her words of love and encouraging her to stay. Instead of him reaching out to her in her love language, he reached out to her in his love language, physical touch. My client got out of the car and began to walk away. Had they both been aware of each other's form of communication, the end result might have been very different.

You must know your personal love language as well as your partners. There is a point in every relationship when life and reality sets in and you will find that your marriage might seem stale or cyclical. Your goal must be to find the passion again by searching new areas within the reality of the relationship. Sometimes, finding the passion as a couple, means identifying personal desires and begin working on your own fulfillment. In turn, you may discover a positive impact on the relationship as a whole. Your marriage is living. If you do not feed it, you risk it dying; dying in the sense of divorce or one spouse feeling unfulfilled and distant. The more authenticity and time you give to your life roles, the more they will be accepting of the time you give to yourself.

Aside from having "positive barriers," we probably have far more "not so positive barriers" that stop us from propelling toward fulfillment. Some examples of the negative types of barriers that we encounter as women are, striving for perfectionism, overeating, procrastinating, being overly critical of oneself, self-medicating via drugs, prescription pills or alcohol, pressuring others for consistent reassurance, or self-injury. Throughout my years as a therapist, I have found that some of the top barriers that stop women from moving forward toward fulfillment are the need to control others, anger and anxiety. This section will discuss these three major types of barriers. There are many more barriers that might stop you from reaching goals and seeking fulfillment. Your goal is to reflect on each of these barriers in depth in order to help you create a plan on how to move through them in the future. Just as Life fulfillment is subjective, so are barriers. Be authentic and honest when identifying these barriers. Knowing your barriers is half of the battle.

One of the most common types of barriers women face is the need to control others. The need for control can be a hard barrier to fess up to sometimes. You only get one key to the car that rides you through the journey of life. Hold that key tight and control your own vehicle. Do not give that key away and let others take control of your journey. Likewise, people have their own keys to their car. Do not try to take control over other people's cars and change their journey, even if you think that you are right. You can provide those you love or "need to change" with a map for their journey, but you cannot drive the car for them. I would suggest reacting to the people you want to change differently than you currently do. If you change the path you are driving, if they want to follow, they will change paths, too. However, for many, your journey and path is not what is right for them. The best way to change a person, is to not change them at all. Rather, change your normal responses to them and they are consequently then forced to change their responses to you.

At my Superwoman workshops, all of the women get a generic key. They are to take the key and mark it or design it. They can put little beads on it, paint it, or simply put a dot on it with a marker. Then, they are asked to put the key on their key ring. Every time they grab their keys, use their keys, etc. they get a quick reminder that they hold the key and control to their lives. I suggest that you do the same. Find an old key and make it your new symbol of self-control. Put it on your key ring as a reminder that you hold the control to your life. Only you get to design this key and make it your own. When you try to control someone else, remember, they have designed their own key, too. Your design, thoughts, actions, values and beliefs are your own. Your key has been created much differently from the way your spouses, friends and coworkers have chosen to design their keys. Don't try to tell others how to design their key to life, where to park, and which car to drive. Whatever you do, don't drive their car. There is way too much responsibility that comes from taking over someone else's car/life. When you are focused on someone else's life, how can you find time to focus on your own Life and fulfillment? Trying to control someone else's vehicle becomes a full time life role. Trying to control someone else sets you up for failure. If you try to control someone who doesn't want to change, your attempts will fail. Unfortunately, you will find that you have put so much effort and time into working on them that you forgot about yourself, decreasing personal fulfillment. I have yet to meet one person that can successfully drive two cars at once.

If needing to control other people is one of your barriers to personal fulfillment, take a moment to really reflect on why you may fear giving up control in certain areas of your life. Do you fear not knowing the end result of something or someone if you are not in control of the situation or person? Think back to delegating out tasks and how the need for control might be a barrier in your ability to do this. Do you worry that things will not turn out "perfect" if *you* don't do them? The reality is, that while women sit around doing everything "perfectly," the one thing that is not "perfect," is our level of fulfillment. If sports practice chauffeur and your career are in your top five life roles, I do not recommend delegating these activities out all the time, but then however, do delegate out dinner, laundry, and other roles that are not in your top five. If dinner and laundry are not in your top five life roles, then don't add on the extra burden that comes behind trying to control the outcome of these activities. Delegate them out and march on to something else worth and deserving of your energy and time.

I have had women tell me that they "have" to do the grocery shopping because their partners never do it right. Apparently, you can get a diploma in grocery shopping and men have not taken the courses to make them eligible to do this task. Guess what ladies, this is where we stop sweating the small stuff and begin delegating out the grocery shopping. There is no degree in Grocery Shopping. Who cares that he brings home a dozen eggs and five of them are broken? You are going to break the eggs anyway when you use them. If he comes home with broken eggs, send him back out to buy more. Trust me, the first few times he has to go out twice for eggs, he will never do it again. Give people time to learn how to complete these tasks. Do not set your expectations for perfection. You might have to teach your spouse, child or friend what to do the first few times, but then after a while, things will get easier when they can carry the weight with you. Teaching takes time initially, but once the lesson is learned, you will find more time for yourself and more comfort in delegating out. Most supports want to help you and might even find contentment and fulfillment in being able to give you a hand here and there. As you release control of other people or the insignificant tasks in your life, you may find that you have more free time to focus on your personal fulfillment.

Honestly ask yourself if you are trying to change someone. Perhaps you are channeling a lot of your time and energy into getting your boss to see that the way he is operating the office is wrong or that your adolescent's "friends" are really not his, "friends." This is control. Remember, you only have one key and that drives your own car. Provide a map to your boss and adolescent, but do not control them. Change your responses, behaviors and thoughts, and that will change those individuals around you. When it comes to children, I understand that it is hard to not be in control. We have lived through what they are currently going through and we are aware of the outcomes, consequences and pains that they will face. We sometimes control to protect. The reality is, parenting and controlling are two different things. That line can be grey, but growing up and making mistakes is part of everyone's journey. You can protect and guide your adolescent, but ultimately, they will make their own choices. If your child makes a poor choice, this is not a direct reflection of you. Rather, poor choices and consequences are a reflection of the trials of life. As you let go of controlling others and refocus your control only onto you, you will begin to find more fulfillment and peace.

I have seen women try to change and control men. Women assume that if they can maintain control over certain aspects of their partner, there is less to fear, less unknown and at some point, "he will come around." Women rationalize by saying "I'm not controlling him, I'm just guiding him." Wrong! When you take your key and try to control someone else's car with it, you are not only setting yourself up for disappointment, but a potential crash. People have to want to change, and they can't just say that they want to change; they have to really want to and believe that they can. It's the whole, "you can lead a horse to water but you can't make him drink," saying. You increase your likelihood of disappointment and reduce fulfillment the more you keep trying to change someone. Patterns of repeated negativity get your brain into the habit of observing more failures as opposed to successes.

For some women, they have so little control over their own lives, that they cling to those who might let her control them. One example is the woman who seeks out the "bad boy." Bad boys need to be "tamed" or "controlled," and a woman who lacks control in herself, is up for the challenge. A woman who pursues the bad boy as her challenge may even take on the motherly role as she mends and molds him. This definitely takes a woman's time and energy. It becomes an entirely new life role to mend, mold and change someone.

Women who have abusive or controlling partners may feel that they have been robbed of their personal self-control. As humans, we have a need and desire to control. Control is okay, as long as we focus on controlling ourselves. If control has been taken away from us, we may find that we are seeking out control in other avenues. In the situation where a woman is in an abusive and controlling relationship, she may find herself overbearing with her children in order to compensate for the lack of control within herself and marriage.

Women with eating disorders also tend to lack control in their lives. Research shows that women who are anorexic perceive control over their lives as minimal, and that their food intake and weight are some things that they can control. When women fail, we hold ourselves very accountable. This increases our self-doubt, decreases our confidence and potentially increases symptoms of depression. The more we realize that we have wasted our energy and time on something or someone that did not change, the longer we cycle on the Ferris Wheel with regret. If control is one of your barriers in pursuing fulfillment, take a moment to reflect on why control is so important to you. Does it come down to fear; perhaps a fear over losing something or someone? Do you lack control in yourself and are trying to regain it by controlling others? Regardless of the reason, take time to search for the answer within yourself. Be authentic. The self-reflection process can be painful and eye opening, but self-awareness could mean self-fulfillment.

Another major barrier that I notice in women is anger. Anger is poison. It makes us do and say stupid things that we regret. When we hold onto anger, we end up hurting ourselves. If you are mad at someone, how are you hurting *them* by sitting and brewing day in and day out about how much *you* are angry? They are going about their lives, taking up more opportunities and living in the moment, while you sit their spending your energy on them. The real way to get back at someone, channel your anger into something you love, and do it! You will be so consumed with LIFE that you will be able to better put into perspective what really matters to you. If someone is making your life miserable, it is only because you are letting them. They have one key, and it goes to their car, do not allow them to put their key into your vehicle and drive it.

Anxiety is a mixed emotion. Anger can stem from anxiety, but can shadow the anxiety as a defense for hiding emotions that are too strong. By getting angry, we now have found a reason to take the blame off of ourselves. Anger not only assists us in finding fault in others, but it eliminates or minimizes the responsibility we should take upon ourselves due to our own errors or insecurities. When we place blame or anger onto someone else, we minimize the chances of our insecurities coming forth. If our insecurities come forth we risk people seeing that we are not who we say we are, and that creates anxiety. We are attempting to direct the attention off of us and onto someone or something else. Placing blame onto someone or something else, other than the source causing pain, is called displacement. Displacement is a defense mechanism used to alleviate anxiety when faced with aggression or anger. An example of displacement is when you come home from being yelled at by your boss and you scream at your husband. You are not mad at your husband, but rather the anxiety and anger your boss provoked is being taken out on your husband. In fact, this is one reason why women should work to compartmentalize problems. When women are at their strongest and most positive, that is the time to form a habit of dividing out problems; what I like to refer to as compartmentalizing. Once you are in a habit of compartmentalizing your issues or problems, then the wrong person will not take blame for someone else hurting you. In the previous example of the boss and spouse, instead of work being the primary problem in this situation, you now have created an additional problem with your spouse, unnecessarily. When you compartmentalize your problems, if you have a bad day at work, you come home and use your spouse as a support system as opposed to a person you can displace your anger on to.

This method of compartmentalizing goes for larger, less surface issues as well. If you were hurt in the past by a lover, it is not fair that your new lover suffers. Compartmentalize these people or your anxieties. Do not hurt someone undeserving, and do not sabotage a relationship with someone who could be a loving and healthy support for you. In taking responsibility for yourself, you must be aware that others, who were not present in the past, should not be responsible for your past. If you are unhappy now, you are either giving someone permission to make you feel this way, or you could be hurting people or things in your major life roles that are undeserving of this pain. You want the people and things that lie within your top five life roles to be happy and strong. If they are not happy and strong, take a look at various aspects of these life roles and check to make sure that you are not displacing unnecessary emotions or pain onto them.

I was counseling a family where the parents were in the middle of a divorce. In session, we processed the divorce and the adolescent boy took the news extremely well. This was in June. Right as the holidays were approaching I noticed a change in this very smart and well behaved boy. He began cursing more, getting upset toward his mother, and having bouts of tears randomly regarding his father. His behavior changed in school and he was acting out more. He became very rude toward his sister. On the outside, the boy was riddled with anger. I tried various anger management techniques and they helped only for the short term. The presenting issue was anger, but I quickly realized anxiety was being masked with anger. I decided to take a different approach and use techniques to talk about what might be causing him anxiety. At first he denied that he was anxious at all. However, as time went on, the boy talked about his pain for not being with both parents at the holidays. He wanted more clarity about how visitations worked. The anxiety from the unknown about upcoming life experiences needed to be addressed in order for the anger to go down.

The point is, if you have emotional pain, you cannot just start treating yourself unknowingly. You have to take time to reflect on the root cause of your pain. This does not necessarily mean that you have to talk about your childhood for years on end, but it does mean you need to take time to self-reflect and understand what pain you are actually feeling. You do not want to misdiagnosis your pain or mistreat it. Doing so is waste of your time and energy, and you risk losing confidence in yourself. If you take time to explore your emotions, you may find that you are masking underlying anxieties with anger. When you are aware of what the root issue is, you will treat yourself differently. As you explore your inner self, you get to know you better. You may find things that excite you, relax you, or even scare you. In the beginning of this book I told you that we were going to embark on a journey toward finding your fulfillment. That is exactly what this is, a journey. You will not find "you" until you are authentic with yourself and discover the root of your pain or non-fulfillment. Being authentic and finding the root of your non-fulfillment can be challenging but this is part of your journey, so take your time.

Anxiety and anger are sometimes seemingly unstoppable barriers. As women, we have anxiety over varying things. It is important to evaluate your anger and anxieties to determine if some of these emotions are stemming from hidden insecurities. If they are, what can you do to alter or address these insecurities? What issues can you compartmentalize? As you question the certainty in some areas of your life, take time to reflect and journal on these aspects. Remember, you cannot change the person or object you are mad at. You have one key and you can drive only your car.

It is my hope that this chapter has helped you to become more aware of barriers or issues that hinder your growth, fulfillment or relationships. Take some time to explore and look at other barriers that might be stopping you from seeking higher fulfillment. Once you are aware of what is stopping you from being more fulfilled, together we will develop a plan to work through the barriers, propelling us toward a better Work-Life Balance. Below, create a list of people, fears, things, ideas, thoughts, etc. that are stopping you from pursuing your Life balance.

What Stops Me from Pursuing My Fulfillment:

1._____

2._____

3._____

4._____

5._____

6._____

7._____

8._____

9._____

10._____

*For a printable version go to: www.typesuperwoman.com and click on the link that says, "SuperWoman Worksheets."

The list you created is called, barriers. Any goal you ever want to achieve in life, expect barriers along the way. This is normal. Have you ever heard the saying "There are no shortcuts to any place worth going?" It's a true statement.

Now that you can visually see, and are a bit more aware of your barriers, you can devise a plan to work through them. A plan of action will help you to avoid being cornered into uncomfortable situations or can assist you in not being bullied by your barriers. When your barriers try to push you back onto the Ferris Wheel, now you will be more conscious of your choice to pay for another ride around.

Below, rewrite your barriers and then write any falseness to them. Sometimes a barrier is our self. Many of us are not authentic and are not honest about our barriers. Perhaps your integrity is on the line because of something you did. I have counseled women who have engaged in infidelity and are suffering from a lack of fulfillment. Being unfaithful takes time and energy and can be a barrier. You have to be honest and account for this when reviewing your "self" and barriers. Some women find themselves doing something unlawful or unethical, and they must account for the pain, time and energy that goes into these activities. Maybe you hold grudges or hang onto the past in an unhealthy way. Whatever your internal barriers may be, you must complete this form authentically in order for these techniques to work. When the women attend my SuperWoman workshops or come to me for coaching, I am honest with them. I advised them that if they try to seek fulfillment based on dishonesty with themselves, they have wasted their time, energy and money. If you don't want to be honest with all the people around you, fine. But the one person you must be honest with is yourself.

When we try to find our path and identify what we want to do and how we want to proceed, we must be aware of the barriers and stressors that are in our pathway. We must also be honest with the amount of time and energy some people, things or life roles take up in our lives. Some women are extremely stubborn and fail to take responsibility for being overbearing, controlling, or downright mean. To peel off the layers of your personal self and find what your core self needs and desires to create fulfillment, you must be authentic. If you do not plan to complete this worksheet in an authentic and honest manner, you are not yet ready to move forward. Please make sure that you are in a place in your life and environment where you can be open and honest, to you.

Plan for Defeating My Barriers:

1. Barrier

_____

What about this barrier is not all true

_____
_____
_____
_____
_____

Next time this barrier rears its ugly head, I plan to do the following

_____

_____

_____

_____

_____

*For a printable version go to: www.typesuperwoman.com and click on the link that says, "SuperWoman Worksheets."

Now that we have explored the barriers that stop us from moving toward fulfillment, we are going to journey forward and address, leaving the comfort zone.

"Peace is a daily, a weekly, a monthly process, gradually changing opinions, slowly eroding old barriers, quietly building new structures." –John F. Kennedy

Chapter 4

Uncomfortable is Most Comfortable

You have taken the time to reflect on your barriers in life. You were authentic in defining your barriers and misbeliefs. You even devised an action plan that you feel safe acting upon once the barriers rear their ugly heads. Moving forward, you already have two potential problems. First, humans are creature of habit. People try to change their actions and behaviors, but easily revert back to old ways. Two, we attempt to implement our plan, but discover that we are not comfortable acting on it.

Being a creature of habit is detrimental to successfully changing behaviors. The best predictor of future behavior is past behavior, and there is a reason for this statement. We are who we are. It is hard to change ourselves and habits. In therapy, I talk with women who try to "change" their partners. It took 35 years to make that man, you cannot change him in six months! They attempt to rationalize a man's behaviors and work effortlessly to teach him how he "should" be. The man tries to improve his behaviors for a few weeks, but his behavior almost always reverts back. Reverting back to old behaviors is not something just men do, it's a human issue.

If you want to move forward, you really have to want to move forward. You have to make a conscious effort in every breath you take if you want to discover a new you. You will have to be highly conscious and aware of all your interactions and experiences during the day to see where you can be more efficient in order to be more effective and fulfilled. You are going to have to drop a role to add a role. Your new role is you. You will also have to be aware of your behaviors and reactions because your focus is on moving forward and not returning to old habits. If you step away from awareness of the self for just one decision, you may find yourself on one more trip around the Ferris Wheel.

Women spend a lot of time being uncomfortable; perhaps to avoid feelings of guilt or the fear we might lose someone. Women are overwhelmed and face anxieties and stressors every day. Depression is also common in women. Whether the depression is caused by hormonal issues or lack of fulfillment, 25% of women will experience depression in their lifetime and only one in five will seek any type of treatment. Women aged 40-60 are under the most stress. Worse, research shows that women in this cohort face frequent and consistent stress. Consistent and chronic stress is detrimental to the body both mentally and physically. When the body faces a stressor, cortisol, adrenaline and other hormones are released into the body. The release of these chemicals is a way for your body to protect itself. When you really do need to fight or flight, your body has the ability to give you a boost that will get you through an attack. There have been stories of people lifting cars off the ground to save their children from a burning vehicle. The boost of adrenaline and hormones puts the body into a sometimes unreal state for protection.

When the fight is over, the body recovers and hormones go back to their appropriate levels.

For women that are faced with living in a fight or flight state every day, the amount of cortisol and other hormones does not drop back to appropriate levels. Hormones remain unbalanced because the body thinks that it needs to be in a fight or flight state all the time. Overexposure to these hormones can lead to anxiety, heart disease, stomach related issues, sleep problems, depression, weight changes, and memory issues. Because women typically nurture and take care of others when they are ill, they attempt to heal themselves when they become sick out of habit. We treat our family and friends when they are ill so frequently, that this behavior of helping and treating literally becomes a habit. The reality is, you might not know what is really wrong with you. Your illness could be psychosomatic or it could be physical. Panic attacks and heart attacks share several of the same symptoms. You might think you can treat your own panic attack, but for sure you can't treat your own heart attack. Heart disease is the leading cause of death among women. Two-thirds of women will not make a full recovery after having a heart attack. You should not treat yourself.

When you are down, you need to call upon your familial supports or even professional ones. I understand that you might fear disappointing your family or coworkers, but relationships are 50-50 and you need to be sure that you give yourself the time and attention that you give others when you are down. Even more challenging, you have to work on not feeling guilty once you do ask for help from your support systems. A 50-50 relationship does not mean that on Monday mornings you carry the weight and then Monday evenings your spouse carries the weight. Fifty- fifty means there might be months that you are head of household, and then your spouse picks it up later in life. For example, if your spouse gets in an accident at work, you may be responsible for picking up more than you normally do. But when he heals, it is his turn to help out and allow you to focus on you. Now is your time to find fulfillment, and that might require your supports picking up their 50% at this point in time. Be cognizant of self-defeating thoughts that trick you into believing your supports won't help you work toward fulfillment. Do not let self-defeating thoughts become a habitual barrier for you and be sure to eliminate faulty thinking that won't allow you to see your situation from a different angle. Use your confidence as aggression for seeking fulfillment and your communal nature to rally up support systems when you are down.

We come from a society where health care has always been focused on fixing the problem. As women, we need to change our own mindset into prevention. Don't let a problem start; prevent it from ever even happening. You may initially feel that you are going to the doctor more frequently, but the visits will be more positive and in the long run, less financially and emotionally expensive. Forget the saying, "don't fix it unless it's broke" and instead "fix it, update it, and take care of it, before it breaks." Some women will sit for days or weeks on end being ill, downing over the counter medication until their body shuts down completely. After harassment from supports, they go in to the doctor, only to find that they have pneumonia. My mother in law had chest pain, jaw pain, shortness of breath and still waited to see a doctor. She is strong. She raised a family and sat through pain of different sorts her whole life, and made it through. Her habit of taking care of others encouraged her to treat this pain, too. It wasn't until the shortness of breath became unbearable that she decided to go to the doctor. She walked into the doctor's office with shortness of breath and out of the doctor's office with an immediate date in hand for triple bypass heart surgery!

Women face so many stressors on a consistent basis that we wear our immune systems down quickly. Research shows that state of mind affects one's state of health. Women need to increasingly become more aware of the tie between body and mind. Women are susceptible to illness because of the consistent and high levels of stress faced. When we are down, we need to seek help. Somehow though, women have conditioned themselves to be comfortable in this uncomfortable state. Remember how we previously discussed completing a project or waiting on something to come through, and God forbid we have a couple hours of downtime, we fill it with Work? This is because we are actually comfortable being uncomfortable. Women will find things to do that will fill this downtime because we are not comfortable just sitting. When we sit, we discover our thoughts, likes and dislikes. This can be a great thing, but sometimes it is scary, too. Plus, we have guilt that riddles us as we sit there knowing we could be doing so much more for the family or work. Actually though, when you sit and relax you are doing a lot for your health and subsequently for your family and career. The healthier and more fulfilled you are, the more time and energy you will have to give to the people or things that mean most to you. When we sit, we actually have the ability to take in the moment. Taking in the moment is something people pay me to teach them. Taking in the moment is a skill and a goal for both women and men alike. You need to work at feeling comfortable alone. I am not talking about being alone and working, but rather alone with yourself. Take time to meditate. Teach your brain to turn off. Can you imagine a moment of silence, let alone a moment of silence when your brain is even quiet?

I have a canal in the back of my yard. The first year I moved to my home, I took it for granted. I loved looking at the canal, but I never experienced it. The second year, I decided to get a kayak. I decided that time for me was necessary, and I was really lucky to have *this* as my backyard. I needed to practice what I had preached. I no longer wanted to take this beautiful waterway for granted, and I also wanted to enjoy more "moments." I do not take hour long kayak rides during the week, because I do have priorities and work, but I use the waterway to experience Life every so often for twenty minutes. I kayak for about ten minutes and then sit. There is dead silence and the sun is looking down on me. When my mind trails off to work, I just tell myself that for these twenty minutes, I am all that matters. I cannot change anything at that moment. That moment will make me stronger in the moments that lie ahead of me that day. Earlier we talked about the importance of being in the moment with a child or spouse when you are giving time to that particular life role. You are a life role, too. When you are alone with you, focus on you. Answering your bosses call while "in the moment" does not count as you time.

Men are really good at keeping a divide between work and life. Things are not the end of the world to them. If laundry did not get done for a week, they are still assured that the sky will not fall upon them. Men don't care if they look fat in jeans, and don't have a mild heart attack when the baby bumps into the table. They fight with friends, and are over it in five minutes and don't sweat a lot of the small stuff. They are happy fishing. Fishing is an activity where they stare at water with a pole in their hands for hours on end, only then to reel up an empty line. They can turn emotions on and off quickly and avoid holding grudges. If we tell our partners about a co-worker at work who is treating us poorly, they give us a solution and expect us to march on. Then, we get mad at them. Reality check, men are actually right in these situations. We should look for more solutions and avoid holding long emotional grudges. Chances are, if the baby tumbles, he will be just fine and you probably do not look fat in those jeans. And, staring at the water with a fishing pole in hand for hours, might just mean that they know how to enjoy the moment.

The less time that you focus on moments in life, the greater chance of depression you have. During coaching sessions and the SuperWoman workshops, I choose to play an activity I like to call, the "brain game." I take a bowl of clean cooked pasta noodles and set it aside. I have the client come up with her own positive and negative statement cards about herself. Then, we put the positive and negative statement cards into a bucket. The client is asked to pull each card during the course of the activity, but only one at a time. When a positive statement card is pulled, she gets an inspirational card to read and take home. When a negative card is pulled, she pours a dark colored spice onto the clean "brain." By the end of the game, the client is able to see how one negative thought at a time, even when added slowly, consumes the brain. How can someone set goals, meet goals and have healthy support systems when their entire brain is consumed with negative thoughts? They can't. Research suggests that people who have depression are more prone to having their brains pick up more negative statements and comments than those who do not have depression. Negativity brews negativity.

Lack of sleep can also impact fulfillment and increase feelings of depression or anxiety. Broken up sleep is painful. The body only really rests and rejuvenates tissues in REM (Rapid Eye Movement) sleep. REM sleep is referred to as the sleep stage where we dream. In REM sleep the body systems and brain are hard at work rejuvenating, while the muscles of the body go into a paralyzed state. We typically move into REM sleep 90 minutes after we have fallen asleep, and then move in and out of REM throughout the night. Have you ever slept for eight hours and woke up tired or not refreshed, but other times you have slept for five hours and felt great? That is because if you sleep eight, ten, twelve hours and you do not get to

REM sleep or do not spend enough time in REM sleep, you have not fully rested your body and tissues. Your body needs time to rejuvenate. If you sleep for five hours, but most of that sleep is deep sleep, you tend to feel more rested.

Some women indicate that they cannot exercise because of time constraints. However, the more you work out, the quicker your body can pull you into REM sleep. For every 30 minutes you work out, your body can pull you into REM sleep 60 minutes quicker. This theory caps out at one hour of workout. If you work out for one hour, your body can pull you into REM sleep two hours earlier. This means that you can net up to an extra hour per day to do whatever you want. If you choose to take that extra time and spend it on work versus Life, that is your choice. Be comfortable with taking this extra time for your personal fulfillment.

Since women are caregivers by nature, we are comfortable with lying in bed staring at the ceiling while everyone else is asleep. We might even get up to clean at midnight, or, write this book. If our children are ill, we pray to take over the flu for them. I have even talked with women clients who sacrifice going to the doctor just to save on a co-pay or deductible. This is no way to live. Your family, career, and top life roles need you and they need you healthy. You need you healthy. Women certainly do have most all the right answers, but for everyone else. We not only don't have the answers when it comes to ourselves, but sometimes, we don't even know the questions we should ask. Unconsciously, and sometimes even consciously, we push ourselves to stay in this uncomfortable state. The state of the Ferris Wheel.

When I work with women clients, I typically begin the first couple coaching sessions with exploring their values and mission statements for their lives. This gets them in the mode of focusing on themselves. This process is very uncomfortable for some women because it is a rarity to spend one hour focusing only on themselves. Instead of being comfortable with being uncomfortable, your upcoming challenge is to be comfortable being comfortable. That means being over-worked, over-spoused, over-stressed and stepped-over, will actually, be over. In order to be successful in doing this, you have to accept yourself fully. This is not always an easy process. You have flaws, you have guilt, you have fears, and you have a past; all things that might constitute as some of your barriers. Addressing all these issues at one time may be a bit overwhelming. In order to have time for Life, you have to let go over some of these issues. Pick one or two issues, and start letting go. If you spend time worrying about the future and complaining about your past, you have no time to enjoy Life in the present. One quote I chuckle at every time, yet is so true, "complaining about complaining, is still complaining."

Grab a note book, and every time you have a fear, guilt, or dwell on the past, put a little tally mark on the paper. At the end of the day, look at how much time you have spent doing these activities. Wouldn't you rather spend your Life doing something else? There is all of this debate on nature and nurture. It is my biological makeup or it is the way my family treated me. These concepts do play a role in who we are, but why blame nature or nurture or why spend your time trying to figure out which one made you ride the Ferris Wheel? Quit placing blame, take responsibility and focus on you. Control and change you.

Reverting back to old habits is easy. Remaining comfortable being uncomfortable is easiest in the short run, but in the long run can be very detrimental to your health and Life fulfillment. You will not only need a plan on how to have a more fulfilling Life, but you will also have to set up a reward system for yourself. When you travel outside of your comfort zone, when you take a risk, when you reach out for support, you get a reward. At first these behaviors will feel awkward, but that is good because the way you have been living has not provided you with all the fulfillment you desire and deserve. Rewarding yourself for traveling outside of your comfort zone is a great way not to feel guilty about doing something for yourself because essentially, you have earned it!

Reward yourself all the time, several times per day. I do not necessarily mean that you get twelve pedicures per day, but reward yourself with something small, but fun. For example, if you take the stairs instead of the elevator, you get that Hershey kiss sitting on your desk, I won't tell. If you work out an extra five minutes you can hit that book store for ten minutes before going home. I notice a lot of the women I counsel want to increase how much water they drink. Together we work to cut out the sodas and introduce more water.

Water lubricates joints and moistens body tissues. It gives the body a better overall feeling. When the women reach their daily goal for water intake, they can reward themselves with something small. Even tea or a cup of coffee in between water intake would suffice as a reward. It is about doing Work, but rewarding with small bits of Life. Think rewards every day, all day. This will get you into beginning a habit of focusing on things you like. It will also help you begin to navigate away from uncomfortable as being comfortable and comfortable being comfortable.

Below is a Bucket List form. When you reach a major goal, reward yourself with something off the list. Get your family involved. Doing something for yourself, while also having family or friends share in it with you, will reduce feelings of guilt and will also foster more love and support. I encourage you to mark off at least four Bucket List items per year. This form is not easy to fill out. We all have our top ten Kick the Can To Do's, but to list out 100, that takes some self-exploration. If you have old journals or diaries from when you were younger, take those out and review them. This will help you to reflect on your inner child and what you had always hoped you would become. Talk to friends, explore magazines, sit at a park or look at old photo albums to help inspire you or assist you in remembering what you wanted out of Life. Here are a couple rules for the bucket list:

1. Every single Bucket List item cannot be to travel somewhere. I am sure we all have 100 different Islands we want to go to

before we kick the can, but listing out 100 different islands to go to is not the point of this activity. Plus, going to five different islands per year would be very time consuming and really expensive anyway!

2. Every single Bucket List item can't be all work related. The point of this activity is to find Life fulfillment. If you want to speak at a conference, write a book, or get promoted to CEO, write that down on your bucket list, but also explore non work related Life goals you have. You are seeking balance.

My Bucket List

Purpose: The purpose of this worksheet is to get you to think about all the things you want to experience and do before you "kick the can." You are encouraged to think of both work AND life goals you have.

Directions: Create a list of 100 things you will do before you die. You must come up with 10 things today and 20 things within one week. Complete the entire list of 100 before the next month's end.

Challenge: You are challenged to at least complete a minimum of four Bucket List items off your list per year.

*For a printable version go to: www.typesuperwoman.com and click on the link that says, "SuperWoman Worksheets."

"First we make our habits, and then our habits make us." –John Dryden

Chapter 5

Success Tracking

In this chapter you are going to track your successes. This may seem tedious or meaningless initially, but when you visually see your progress, you will be consciously, and more importantly, unconsciously, motivated to keep moving toward your goals. Did you know that 90% of people who write down their goals will reach their goals? For heaven's sake, put those goals on paper, the odds are in your favor!

Have you ever watched a child play video games? When they see that they have won a level, and are immediately advancing to the next level, they keep going. If the game did not tell them that they had won, they might be more inclined to stop playing or to "come back to it later." I want you to think a similar when way it comes to setting your goals. There truly is a difference between having goals in your head and actually writing them out and seeing your progress. Once you can visually see your progress and that the gates are open to the subsequent level, you walk right into the next step up without even knowing. There are probably many goals you have reached over the years that you never wrote down. However, when you write out your goals, you will find that you will strive harder and more efficiently to achieve that goal quickly. You want to check that "task" off your list. Once you obtain a goal and see that you have achieved it, you will find a boost of confidence that propels you into setting another goal immediately. All of these behaviors bring you closer to self-actualization and fulfillment.

Before you begin tracking your progress, there are a few ground rules. Most importantly, think positive. As you move toward your goals and fulfillment in Life, there will be bumps, bruises and barriers. That is life. Life is a journey, and so is finding fulfillment. Bumps are a part of the journey; sometimes they even make fun memories. The catch here is that you have to think positive in good times and in tough times. Also, you really have to believe in this whole theory that thinking positive will bring positivity and goodness to you. If you just say that, but you don't believe it, it does not work. This is similar to the people who say they want to change, but don't really want to change; they never end up actually changing. When you really believe that good things are coming, you set yourself up and do things that will bring positivity into your life.

Have you ever met those people who their lives seem to be awesome? Good things happen to them, one thing right after another. They are the ones whose children are always doing well in school, their cars never break down, and they are promoted every year! If something does come up in their lives that constitutes as negative, it doesn't seem to crush them. Now, have you met those people who you almost feel bad for them? They just can't seem to catch a break in their lives. Their child is always sick, their hitching rides to work because their car broke down again, and they deserved the promotion but never got it. It's one negative thing after another.

They live their lives in crisis mode, every day. Here is the difference. Life is a bunch of ups and downs for everyone. If life and its journey were laid out, it would look like this:

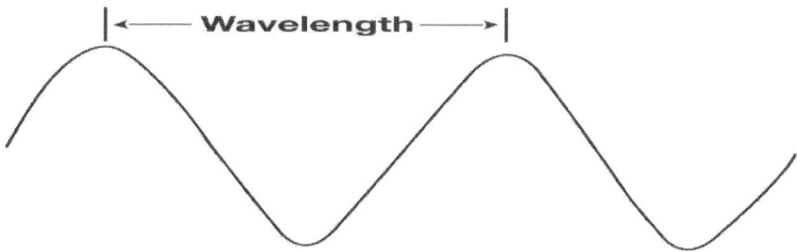

The difference between the people who always seem to "have it good" and the people who "can't get a break" is that those who "have it good," make decisions in life at high points. If you are in a depressed state, angry state, going through a divorce, failing at something, a family member died, you lost your job, whatever the case may be, you are not ready to make a major Life decision. When you are going through something major, and what might constitute as a low point in your life, there is probably a lot of emotion behind the issue. When emotion becomes dominate in decision making, often times it is not the right decision. It is a decision made out of spite, revenge, anger, and not clear mindedness, analysis or basic commonsense. This is why some of the best business savvy individuals are so successful. They do not make decisions based out of emotion. We might deem these types of business individuals as mean or heartless. Perhaps they chose to let go of a single mother who is late to work three times per week but is also trying to juggle children, work, school and a divorce on her own. Her anxiety and depression are forcing her to live in crisis mode. Quite frankly, I do agree that letting this single mother go constitutes as mean, but on the other hand, it might be a good business decision for the company. This woman may be costing the company a lot of money and time and her behaviors might rub off onto other employees who think that if she can come in late, so can they. When I say to you, I think this boss is "mean" for firing the single mother, I am coming from a place of emotion. I am upset or angered by the boss's decision to not understand her life situation. If the boss made decisions based out of emotion and thinking about how everyone else would feel, it is likely that the business would not be as successful.

People who live in crisis mode are forced to make decisions based out of emotion. Then this pattern of bad choices and decisions cycles their self-esteem down and their self-doubt up. When you make an incorrect decision, you have put yourself right in line with being forced to make another choice or decision that is not positive; hence, one bad decision after another, or never getting a break in life. Those that think positive and make decisions at high points in their lives, set themselves up for making a second positive decision and so on and so forth. If someone who has mostly positive days and positive thoughts hits a bump in the road, they have stored so much energy that they can battle the barrier with limited force and still win. Those that live in crisis mode deplete their energy every day and have nothing in storage for when a major crisis hits.

The brain, in a resting state, consumes approximately 20% of your body's energy. Thus, in a clear minded, and resting state you are expending energy. When we are in crisis mode, expect to expend at least double or triple the amount of energy as those individuals not in a crisis. I tell all my clients that they get 20 energy dollars per day. Use them wisely. If you only had twenty dollars to use each day, you would choose what you spent your money on wisely. You would focus on what counts and matters most to you and your family. Would you spend five of your twenty dollars on buying someone else shoes? No! So do not spend your energy dollars on feeding into someone's gossip at work or holding grudges. Take your energy dollars and spend them on what matters to you and your Life.

I guess the million dollar question then is how do you stay positive in a negative situation or how do you begin to believe in this whole theory of "if you think positive, positive things will come?" The trick is in reframing the situation. Every bad situation has a light or a different way to see what has happened. Even if you have to reframe something devastating as a learning lesson, this will help you to move forward. If we sulk, we hinder our forward progress. If our progress is hindered, we stay in the spot we are in, anger or sadness. This is not to say that when it comes to losing someone due to a death or divorce that we do not grieve. Grieving is actually a natural and healthy process. People should grieve, and should take the time to engage in this process so their bodies can work to heal.

First, let's examine a situation that is not a death. Some women are unhappy in the career that they are working in. If you acknowledge that you have a choice in working there, the situation immediately becomes lighter because ultimately you do have an out. You are not bound by law to work there. It may not be easy to leave this particular job for various reasons, but the very fact of believing you could leave gives the mind peace. You have options. They may not be all the options you like, but at least you have some choices.

If you have decided that you are not going to leave your job, you must accept your decision. Do not make every day of your working life miserable. You have chosen to stay. Avoid brainwashing yourself via gossip with coworkers about how horrible the workplace is to work in. Not only does gossip help to consistently reiterate to the brain that your job is unfulfilling, but you will also begin to associate yourself with people who support your view or fuel your fire. This validates the negative workplace. Even more, bosses and managers observe this behavior. This type of behavior may lead to a loss of advancement opportunity which may have put you in a position to enjoy your career.

If you work really hard in your career, but feel you are not noticed, instead of blaming authorities, look at yourself and what you can control. Once you are in control of what is happening to you, you will find that you can make changes to help promote yourself. If your boss doesn't notice you, you have put the control onto his/her plate and thus you have no recourse, so you are pretty much at a standstill. However, if the promotion did not come through because of something you did or did not do, you now have the control to change this. So, what can you do? You work hard, avoid gossip and are definitely qualified for a promotion. Speak up. Have you gone to the correct people and departments to show off your work? Have you marketed yourself to them? Sell yourself. If you sit back, someone else will snatch the opportunity. If someone else got a promotion over you look at what characteristics they have that you lack. What do they perform better at? Ask mangers what you can do to improve and how. Ask for more leadership roles. If someone unfairly received a promotion, maybe it is time to look in other areas of the company or outside the company for promotional opportunities. Maybe you have to go a longer route and go back to school or take extra trainings. Regardless, you have choices and have control and you must reframe each situation in order to begin to believe that positive thinking creates a positive life. Choices are not always easy to make and sometimes our choices mean choosing between the lesser of two evils. The point though, is you have a choice. With every choice, comes a choice in how you choose to act or react. Viktor Frankl said it best "We all have the ability to choose our attitude in the midst of difficult circumstances."

Think about a situation where you are placing blame on someone else. Even if you think, or "know" that the situation is "their" fault, how can you take control for your actions in the situation? What can you change? How would your life be better if you took responsibility for some of the situation? How would your life be different if you began implementing change? Remember, you only get one set of keys to life, and those keys are to drive your own car. You cannot change someone else, even if you spend your life trying. You can though, change your responses and thoughts, which will change those around you.

Finding positivity in devastating situations such as death or divorce can be challenging. Let's use death of a loved one for our example. How could one find something positive with a spouse that has passed away? Initially, there is probably nothing positive, and feelings of hopelessness, especially if children are involved, will linger. This is a normal feeling. You have to grieve, and there may be situational depression involved, rightfully so. However, time heals. The fact that time heals may have to be the focus of every day after a spouse dies. It is not to forget the spouse, but to know that time will help you to cope and move on. Life forces you to march on whether you want to or not.

To remain positive during a death or divorce, avoid making additional major life decisions. Earlier we discussed the wave length of life. Death and divorce are some of the lowest points in a person's life and we should not make decisions at this point. If you focus on getting through the pain, as opposed to adding on more life changes, when you make your way out of grieving, you will come out with less problems. When you make decisions based on emotions, at low points, or impulsively, in the long run, you might find that you have more problems to manage than you initially had. When you give time a chance to heal or you let the emotion lessen, you now can begin to make decisions in a more positive state which will lead to more positive decisions.

Sometimes after a divorce or death we are forced to make decisions, such as what to do with children, money or moving. If you must make a decision, be sure to seek support from those around you as well as professional assistance. It is hard, but even in heartbreaking times, you have to be strong enough to write down and analyze your options. This is where you need to call upon your confidence. In situations where you think you only have one option, you need to take time to reflect on the event and find a second option. This is reframing. Chances are, in most situations there is more than one choice for you. Thinking from other perspectives allows for more choices and the potential availability of more positive outcomes.

Look back at a time in your life when you lost someone or something close to you. How did you learn from that situation? Moving forward, when you lose something or someone close to you, how do you plan to behave or react differently? What were some of your strengths in this situation? How can you use these strengths in other areas of your life? What is something that you did not know about yourself until this even occurred?

As you track your progress, here is ground rule number two, do not compare yourself. You are you. You are not him, you are not her.

You can improve, change, adapt, but you still won't be him or her. Have you ever met someone who is trying to be someone else? They try to look or act like this other person and it seems out of character or it just doesn't fit. We are amused at how hard they try to be someone else, because they never actually will be this other person. The time and energy they expend on comparing themselves is reducing their chances of becoming self-actualized and fulfilled.

We see this behavior in adolescents. They try to be someone from a favorite television show, or try to act like the "popular" girl. We all tried to act like someone at one time or another, but the one thing that we found, we could not actually be them. Thus, it is not fair to step on someone else's scale of Life when you are measuring yours. This does not mean that you cannot have role models and mentors. You can admire certain characteristics in people such as their motivation or integrity. You can use certain people's life paths as a guide to help you. You can mimic fashion styles. The one thing you cannot do is become someone else. Their past is different, their biology is different, and there is a lot you do not know about them. You are in control of you and need to take the time and energy to explore who you are before you can rate yourself up against someone else, who in reality, you might really not even want to be. When you compare yourself, you put yourself in a direct line for failure and feelings of guilt. Take for example when we try to keep up with Mrs. Jones, and we can't, we have guilt. How does she do it? What am I doing wrong? Will my children suffer? Is my husband happy? Kindness might not equal doormat but comparing yourself to others does equal failure and guilt. No comparing.

I tried to keep up with the Jones's. Mrs. Jones puts her kids to bed at 7:30 pm if you didn't know that. My children are up well past that. I found myself upset that the children were up until ten! What kind of mother am I? Actually, when I stopped comparing myself to Mrs. Jones, who I don't even personally know, I found out, I'm a great mother. My husband and I both work from home. I get to take my oldest to school and pick him up every day. He is academically and behaviorally doing very well. On busy days, when I am not around to see the boys, I bring my computer to the bed and work while they lie next to me and watch cartoons. I work in bed with the boys well past 7:30 pm. But reality is, what I am doing, is what works for my family and makes us successful.

As you begin to rate your progress, you need to think about your personality type and what will get you visually or mentally stimulated to continue moving forward. One way to track your progress is using a likert scale, (number line 1-10). For example, let's say your goal is to improve your overall mood. Each week you track your mood on a scale from 1-10, one being a depressed and negative mood, and ten being the best possible mood you could have. As you track your weekly mood, you also journal so that you can pinpoint why some weeks your mood was at a five and others an eight. You can reflect back in your journal to see if hormones played a role in your mood, interactions with certain people, lack of exercise, eating or certain thoughts. If you can reflect on your behaviors through reviewing journal entries, you have the awareness and control to change some of your actions or thoughts. This should lead to more frequent highs in regard to your mood on your likert scale.

Sometimes our barriers are not always obvious to us. You may think that you do not fear anything or that you do make decisions at high points. However, when your experiences and interactions are written down on paper and you can go back at a later date to reflect on your behaviors and thoughts, you have created an entirely different situation for your brain. Your brain has had time to reflect on situations and events in your life as an outsider. You are the third party reflecting on an event from the past. When you go back to things at a later time, you have a stronger and a clearer head to work with; a head with less emotion, less negativity and more common sense. This is a similar concept to not making impulsive decisions. People who are impulsive tend to react, retreat, and then rethink. You want to retreat, rethink and then react. When you take time to reflect on the issue, you are more aware of the reality of the situation. In your journey toward self-fulfillment, you want to avoid having biases against other people and work to acknowledge your flaws. You do have flaws, and that is okay. When you reflect on your progress and your journal writings, be open and authentic to what you observe. You may discover that you are a very critical person of others or that you are avoidant or lack boundaries. Knowing is half the battle, it's true.

Perfection is non-existent. People who claim that they are perfectionists often don't find fulfillment when they reach their goals. When a perfectionist does fail, they are very critical of themselves leading to self-defeating beliefs and a reduction in confidence. This discourages them to reset new goals decreasing the potential for fulfillment. Those trying to seek perfection will only cycle at the point in life they are at, whereas those who acknowledge flaws can find ways to fix them and move forward toward self-actualization. Self-actualization means to develop your full potential. You can be fulfilled in Life, but you are never 100% self-actualized. This would mean you are perfect, and you can always be become better. People do not want to associate with people that think they are "perfect." People who accept their flaws are aware that they are not perfect and will not be able to live up to your standards, so they stay away. Trying to be perfect, or thinking you have to be perfect, sets you up for failure. If perfection does not exist and you are striving for something nonexistent, the odds are not in your favor. Since life is subjective, if perfection did exist, what was perfect to me, would not be perfect to you. This is why you do not want to spend your life trying to please other people because your definition of being perfect for them is different from their definition.

In coaching sessions, I make use of a thermometer as a method to track progress. Here is how the thermometer tracker works. On a sheet of paper make a thermometer without all the dashes. On the very top of the thermometer you write your ultimate goal. The goal must be dated, realistic and achievable. For example, the top of the thermometer could read "Get into Graduate School for Business-September 2014." Each week, you create smaller goals that must be achieved within that week. Week one's goal might be to "research top business schools" and "select a date to take the GMAT prep course." At the one week mark, assuming you have reached your goals for that week, you will begin to color up the thermometer closer to the goal line. Your thermometer is equally divided out into sections based upon your goal start date and end date. Each week you color in that particular section achieved and you will begin to see your thermometer raise closer to the finish line. I suggest that each week you reach your goals you provide yourself with a reward. Do not short yourself and miss a week of rewards. Giving rewards encourages the brain at both conscious and unconscious levels to create healthy habits.

You may have created your own tracking system or researched one you like. Here are some questions you will need to ask yourself as you begin to track your progress: What is my concrete and identifiable goal? How many goals will I set? How do I plan to rate my progress? What will I set as time frame to complete these goals? Are the goals too vague? How will I know if I have reached the goal?

This chapter is a never ending chapter. That is because you will always rate your progress on the different goals you work toward. When you meet one Life goal, you will be aligned with an opportunity to begin working toward another Life goal. Which at that time, you will come back to this chapter and rerate your progress. As we strive to become better every day, we are stepping closer to self-actualization.

"We all want progress, but if you're on the wrong road, progress means doing an about-turn and walking to the right road"
- C.S. Lewis

Chapter 6

Defining my Goal

Get a grip! I mean, get a goal. Goals are important to have because it helps us work toward fulfillment. Without strong goals, we assume that "cleaning the house" or "making it through the work week" is our goal. Making it through the work week is important, but those types of goals contribute to the day to day life routine goals that keep us on the Ferris Wheel. Those goals are more like to-do's for the week, as opposed to long term goals that personally fulfill us. We all have to-do's. In fact, we have to have to-do's. To-do's get us through the week and keep us organized. However, we are not to confuse to-do's with Life goals. A clean house doesn't lead to Life fulfillment, it is more of an immediate sense of satisfaction. It is very important that you know the difference between a to-do and a goal. To-do's keep us on the Ferris Wheel, goals get us off.

There have been cognitive explanations as to why goal setting is effective. The theory is that when we set goals there becomes a discrepancy between what we currently have and what we want. This discrepancy causes a sense of dissatisfaction. When we have unfulfilled goals, our brain has intrusive thoughts about the goal until it is fulfilled. The dissatisfaction with our current state creates an incentive for us to try and change our situation, thus we attempt to respond to the discrepancy by working toward our goal.

In order to successfully reach goals that we set for ourselves, we must set goals that are specific, measureable and attainable. Think of the acronym S.M.A.R.T. when setting goals. S.M.A.R.T. stands for specific, measureable, attainable, relevant and time-bound. Having personal or professional support systems holding you accountable to your goals also increases your chances of being successful. If you do not have strong support systems or are not seeing a professional to help guide you toward fulfillment, be sure to hold yourself accountable by setting up reward systems.

Thinking or verbalizing your goals is not enough. Goal setting is an art. It takes self-reflection and time to create effective and measurable goals. If you have not reached goals in the past, reflect on the potential reasons why. If your goal is too broad you are setting yourself up failure. For example, "My goal is to take over the world." This goal is not specific enough to be achievable. What in fact do I want to take over in the world? This goal is not measureable. How will I measure when I have taken over the world? My goal is also not attainable or realistic. With all of the security in the world, and people having control over their own lives, chances are, I won't be able to "take over the world." If you do not set specific, measureable and attainable goals, you add more barriers to the road you are walking down. You are already going to encounter bumps on your journey toward success, do not create unnecessary barriers from the start. Start your journey out on a strong, clear and focused path. This will increase your confidence and keep you pushing toward your goals when times do get rough.

You can also decrease your chances of being successful when you create goals that are focused on perfectionism or what others want. Women are tough on themselves when they do not succeed. Confidence can quickly be depleted from one or two attempted and unachieved goals. This pattern of striving to achieve and failing is taken personally and is internalized quickly. A lack of confidence impacts moving forward with future goals which in turn hinders fulfillment and increases a woman's chances of depression. Research shows that individuals who are depressed tend to create goals that are less specific. Goals derive motivation and an importance to life and the future. Without clear and specific goals, a future may not seem bright, fulfilling or worthy.

People do not achieve their goals and lack fulfillment when they give themselves unrealistic expectations and compare themselves to others. If your goal in Life is to go back to school and get your Master's degree, you cannot gauge the time and energy that a friend put into her goal and use that as your marker for success. Look at your life only when setting goals. Review your barriers. Do you have children? Do you have a full time job? Is this your first time back in school after ten years? Your circumstances are different from everyone else's. That is why Life is subjective to each person. We all have had, and will have, different journeys. Give yourself realistic deadlines and milestones so that you do not get discouraged and quit. You want a somewhat seamless transition from one Life goal to another so that achieving your Life becomes a habit. Think video game. Think getting off the Ferris Wheel. Think fulfillment.

Here is an example of a specific, measureable and attainable goal. My goal is to finalize my first book by January 2014. This goal is specific. It states what I want to do and by when. I can measure when it is completed based upon how many chapters are finished and having my book proofed and published. My goal is also attainable. Giving myself a year to complete a book is something that can be done and has been done. If I wanted to complete my book in one week, that would be unattainable for me because I cannot commit to the amount of time it would take to write a book in one week. Some people can write a book in one week, but I am not comparing myself to them. Based on my life and what I know I can do and will stick to, this is attainable. Pace yourself. Life is a journey. Enjoy it.

When setting goals you must be sure not to overwhelm yourself. I suggest that you when you have identified your goals, you select two that you want to strive for at a time. If you select two goals to work toward you can generate balance. You are not focused solely on one task in your life nor are you spread too thin. Over the years I have counseled clients who have overwhelmed themselves with tasks, goals and familial matters. Overwhelming yourself with too many tasks and goals can create anxiety. Some people with high levels of anxiety find themselves having panic attacks. Panic attacks are unexpected episodes of fear that lead to physical reactions when no danger is apparent. Panic attacks come out of the blue and are spontaneously. You might be walking the dog, cooking dinner, relaxing on the couch or reading a book when a panic attack suddenly occurs. Why would someone have a panic attack when reading a romance novel? There is no exact cause for a panic attack, but panic attacks do tend to occur when a person has had a build-up of stressors and emotions. Some people think they are having a heart attack or nervous breakdown. Your body and mind work together. Even as a strong team, the body and mind can only handle so much negativity and stress. Goal setting should be exciting not stressful.

Think about the following scenario. You are holding a flat glass plate in the palm of your right hand. In your left hand, you have one cup of water. Now, pour the water slowly onto the plate. At first, you might notice that the plate is doing rather well holding all this water. However, as the water fills past the little crevice of the plate, you notice that the plate is harder to balance and you begin having doubts that the plate may not be able to continue holding the water. Still, I ask you to pour more water. You know it is not a good idea, but you choose to take more water and add it to your plate. Suddenly, you have added so much water that water is pouring over the edges of the plate. The plate became overwhelmed and the water barreled over, much like a panic attack. If you continue adding to your personal plate in life, at some point your emotions will pour out.

The mind and body must release extreme levels of stress. During a panic attack our emotional stress comes out in a physical mess of sweat, heart palpitations, shortness of breath, terrifying thoughts and a numbing sensation over the body. Women are twice as likely to get a panic attack when compared to men. Panic attacks in women typically start around young adulthood. We begin college, start a career, get married and have children. Very quickly our life goes from 0-60. The body needs time to adapt to these changes. With the changes in our lives come new goals and ventures. Setting professional, personal and academic goals and working to achieve them all at once can be overwhelming for the body. If you set more than two or three life goals, it is up to you to find little ways to release your pain and stressors that will arise each day. Even if you have a great day, journal or reward yourself, do something as a release. Even the good stress, eustress, can be overwhelming for the body. Getting promoted or having a child is wonderful and exciting, but it adds a weight to the body that was not there before. To avoid feeling overwhelmed as you work toward goals, you must create healthy ways to release your emotions.

If working toward two goals can be overwhelming at times, working toward five or six goals can create extreme anxiety and stress. I have worked with overachievers who come into session with five or six major life goals that they plan to work toward. Although it is wonderful to have lots of goals, what is not smart, is trying to reach all your life goals at once. When you tackle too much at once, a sense of being overwhelmed will shut you down, increasing your chances of depression and lack of fulfillment. You might also find that when you create too many goals, even if they are aimed at creating your fulfillment, you are spread too thin. When you add a life role you have to drop one. If you are overwhelmed with more than five life roles, imagine adding the pain from depression or anxiety to the mix, it is like adding two more unnecessary life roles. At some point, your body will shut down or put you into a panic attack state.

My neighbor's mother is about 60 years old. She came into town to help her son move. She didn't want to help, but her son and daughter in law are expecting a baby and she knew that they needed her support for this move. She took on activities that increased her already high levels of anxiety and stress. She doesn't like flying, she flew, lifting was hard for her, but she lifted boxes anyway. During her stay here, I had the opportunity to talk with her about some of her stressors. She doesn't have many stress outlets, doesn't like where she currently lives, and is in too much pain to get out of the house for walks. A few weeks before moving her son, she decided to let a family member live with her until she got on her feet. As we were talking, she realized that she needs to begin focusing her energy on herself before she can focus on all these other life roles. To decrease anxiety and depressive symptoms she must think about which life roles are her priority and give focus to those. For instance, if the grandchild is now a priority, adding on the stress of having another person living with her is not ideal. Changing your living arrangements will add stress, panic and potential health problems. When setting goals, do not overwhelm yourself, pushing you into a fight or flight state.

As you set Life goals, be authentic in regard to the amount of time it will take to complete a Life goal, just do not consume yourself with every little detail of time and energy that it will take. Enjoy the learning and growth process/journey. If you start looking at how many text books you will buy over the course of four years, how many chapters you will have to read each night and then begin creating scenarios that might not even exist, you are being self-defeating. Being self-defeating is a barrier. When you begin working toward a major Life goal, it is really easy to get yourself to shut down and walk away. If you set a Life goal that will lead you toward fulfillment, don't give up or give in. March through the uncomfortableness.

Having support systems is essential when we try to reach goals, especially Life goals. In order to get your supports to "buy" into you seeking out fulfillment, you first truly have to believe you can attain your goals. It goes back to having confidence. The goal you set has to be attainable for your unique lifestyle and you must believe you can achieve the goal. Confidence will be your aggression to fight through your barriers and negative self-beliefs. Do not get people involved in something that you are not going to commit to or do not have the means to complete.

Going back for your MBA or writing a book is something that you can't do alone. You may sit through all your MBA classes alone, but you need people who believe in you and can encourage you to keep going when you want to give up. You also need people who are accepting of you taking time for you. Your supports should understand and accept that time away from them will be taken while you push toward fulfillment. Working toward a life goal may take away from your time allocated to your top five life roles, which probably contain some support systems that you will be calling on to help you. Remember to treat your supports with respect and give them the time they need so you can take the time that you will need. Giving supports your time and energy that they desire will decrease pain that they may feel during this change. The more satisfied your supports systems are with the attention you provide to them, the less guilt associated with personal fulfillment you will feel.

If you find that you cannot deter from your feelings of guilt when working toward a goal, create a second goal that will make you a stronger or more positive person for your life roles. For example, if you are a wife that can be overly critical with your husband, create a personal goal to start becoming a more accepting wife. Set goals and rewards just like you would for your other Life goal. The more satisfied you and your top life roles are, the more effective you will become at completing your Life goals and day to day tasks. You will find that you have less guilt because you will have spent time with your life roles as they perceived as quality time. If you and your top life roles are satisfied, you now have permission to set more goals. Soon, setting goals and becoming efficient, becomes a habit.

When setting goals, you want your support systems to be honest with you. It is better that your partner let you know when you are getting off track rather than having your boss or other people in the community tell you. Being able to accept constructive criticism can be really hard at times. Women like to be right. If we are working on self- improvement, we may need our partners to tell us what we need to work on. Be receptive and really examine the feedback people give you on your "self" and your performance. Do not take the feedback too personal or get outraged. There is a difference between someone being overly critical and hurtful, and those who help you identify weaknesses and encourage you to work through them. The people that lie within your top five life roles, their opinions and feedback should be taken seriously. People's opinion outside of that circle should be acknowledged and then assessed for its worth.

If criticism has intensified emotions and pained you in the past, first identify who provided you with the criticism. Is this person someone you respect and whose opinion you value? Or, is this a person you handed over your key to and allowed them to control your emotions? If so, take your key back today. If criticism has hurt you in the past and it came from a valuable support, perhaps it is time to complete an honest reflection of yourself and see where their feedback might be stemming from.

Achieving a life goal is a big deal. It is a big deal because achieving life goals do not happen overnight and they are not easy to accomplish. To-do's do happen overnight and are fairly easy to accomplish. I can clean the house in one day, I can complete a project for work in one day, I can exercise in one day. I can't get an MBA in one day, write a book, or change all of my negative habits. Self-improvement and achieving life goals takes a long time. That's why Life is called a journey and not a two day vacation. Miley Cyrus sang a song called *The Climb.* The lyrics read "Always gonna be an uphill battle, sometimes I'm gonna have to lose. Ain't about how fast I get there, ain't about what's waitin' on the other side, it's the climb." Enjoy your climb. Every day, as long as you are trying, you are moving up. Even when you hit a bump and appear to be moving backwards, you are still on a climb up. Patience is a skill; lack of patience is a barrier. Fulfillment begins with the first step of our journey and continues to grow as we choose healthy paths for ourselves. Life fulfillment is going to creep up on you during your journey toward your goal. The people you will meet, the self-confidence that will emerge and the self-improvement and knowledge that you will gain are going to give you unexpected long term fulfillment. The personal goal might be to obtain a Master's degree, write a book, or receive a promotion, but there are things you do not know yet that will also lead toward your fulfillment that come from the journey toward your goal.

Defining your goal may be easy to moderately difficult on the rating scale, however, the journey toward obtaining the goal is usually difficult. Don't let your barriers stop you from achievement. Obtaining a goal takes strength. Strength from all systems, mind and body, are required in goal attainment and Life fulfillment. Imagine the following scenario. You put your back up against a wall and hold one leg up in the air. Your goal is to hold your leg up in the air for 30 minutes. This goal is measureable and attainable. It is by far not an easy goal to obtain, but it can be done. When you first put your leg up in the air, you may find that it is somewhat easy to do so. After a short bit, you may find that it takes more systems in your body to keep your leg up. Your stomach and back are now playing a role in this achievement. You are now encountering barriers. Your leg is shaking and you are not even sure that this is the goal you wanted to work toward. You have self-doubt. You also lack confidence that you will be able to keep your leg up in the air for the full amount of time. You need some support to help you keep your leg up. Ask a support person to hold your leg. I did not say that you had to hold up your leg up, alone.

You encountered barriers and instead of giving in, you found a way around it and moved up toward your goal. It is not easy to hold your leg up in the air for 30 minutes, but ultimately, if you want to bad enough, you can find a way to do it. You just have to use other resources and come up with solutions to barriers in order to reach your goals. When you want to give up on a goal, reflect back on why you ever started. People say it is easy to quit. I think the hardest thing to do is quit. The hard part about quitting is the regret and long term lack of fulfillment. When women think about quitting or actually quit, they have guilt or anxiety about giving up. These feelings are painful. Sometimes, regret for not finishing a Life goal lasts days, weeks, months, years or even a lifetime. Passion and hope start you on just about any journey. When you want to give up on your goals, pull out old journals out and reflect on them, talk to support systems, look at old photos and ponder on thoughts as to why you even began this particular journey. Think about what you want for your long term fulfillment. Goals can be set and revised as you hit hurdles and bumps. When you are strong and in a positive place, create ways to spark up your passion, that way, whenever your barriers get the best of you, you can march on toward fulfillment.

If you really want to feel fulfilled, be open to accepting that the journey is not going to be easy, but don't fear that it won't be easy either. Fear of failure will lead you down a non-fulfilled life path. As you move toward fulfillment you are moving up in the self-actualization process. Going up is not easy. Riding a bike up a hill is not easy. Holding your leg up in the air for 30 minutes is not easy. Even driving a car uphill requires more energy from the car. The engine has to work harder altogether to pull you up that hill. Anything that goes uphill takes more strength. Remember grandpa's stories of walking to school in the snow everyday barefoot and uphill? That was not easy for him! The point is, going downhill is easy. Going backward is also easy because you know what to expect, you've been there before. If you want to go forward, you can't be looking backwards. If moving up is tough in almost every situation, do not think that as you move up toward goal attainment that it will be easy. However, when you climb a mountain, and you finally make it to the top, you get to look around at everything that you accomplished. Look at the horizon, look at the base of the mountain where you took your first steps, look at everything between your feet and the start line. That's the journey. All of that led up to this moment of fulfillment. Breathe in the new found confidence. Look at the barriers and fears that you left behind. Look where you finally stand. The journey toward fulfillment isn't going to be easy, but it will be worth it.

"If you don't know where you are going, you'll end up someplace else." -Yogi Berra

Chapter 7

It's Not Only Ok to Ask for Help, It's Mandatory

As we have discussed, you need support systems in your journey toward fulfillment. When you begin to seek fulfillment, you might discover support systems in people that have been there all along that you never turned to. In life, we need support systems. No one is strong enough to get through it all alone. Thinking you are strong enough to do it all alone, could lead to anxiety, depression and health related problems. Marilyn Monroe said "A woman can't be alone…A man and a woman support and strengthen each other. She just can't do it by herself." I certainly do not think every woman needs a man, but, if I could revise and update this quote it would read like this: "A woman needs support systems. Support systems strengthen the already strong woman. No one can get through life alone. We all need support." Life is about balance and that includes balance or 50-50 in relationships.

One thing I have learned from single mothers is that it is okay to ask for help. Single mothers do not fear reaching out for an extra hand. The ability to ask for help and set feelings of guilt aside makes these women stronger, more efficient and more productive. It truly does take a village to raise a child. There is a reason this quote was created. If it took one person to raise a child, the quote would read, "it takes one person to raise a child." The reality is, you can't do everything alone. Select any goal you have and I will tell you that at some point, you will need support to achieve it. You do need help and support systems, single mother or not. You are still a Super Woman if you ask for help. The more help you use, the more Super you will become. Do not be too prideful, fearful or shy to ask for help.

Many mothers struggle to ask for help. Society has a pretty effective way of making women feel guilty if they are not commuting 14 children to 10 different sports games all while making a five course dinner and having the children in bed before 9pm. Who cares what the Jones' say!? Remember, we are not comparing ourselves. You do not know the Jones'. Maybe they have an onsite nanny, have a crappy marriage or hate sports altogether. Or, maybe, they really are happy transporting these children around town. The real reason doesn't matter. Don't waste your time trying to figure their lives out. The Jones' should not be one of your top five life roles. March on in a direction that is good for you and your family. That means, if a mature and supportive neighbor can watch the children while you go to that art class you have wanted to go to, let them. You are still a good mother if you do stuff for yourself; in fact, you are a better mother when you do things for yourself.

The more you put on your plate, the higher likelihood you are to break down. We talked earlier about anxiety and panic attacks. A high level of anxiousness takes energy and time. Anxiety literally becomes a life role. Being anxious and overwhelmed by all the roles you put on your plate, takes a lot of time and attention that you might not have. Women even worry about how much they worry. If you try to "do it all," and even worse, "do it all" by yourself, you have just written yourself a prescription for anxiety. If seeking out help and supports will increase your fulfillment and make your life easier, do it. Do not let society manipulate you into thinking you should do things a certain way. Do not let your assumptions about other people's perceptions impact decisions you make for your family. You do not get an award for "doing it alone." The only thing you get when you overwhelm yourself and do things alone is an increase in anxiety.

Earlier we discussed barriers to our fulfillment. One of the barriers we discussed was perfectionism. A perfectionist thinks that they have to do everything, and do it alone, in order for it to turn out "perfect." If you are striving to be perfect, you put yourself in a position where you are stuck doing everything alone. You are forced doing everything alone because what you perceive is perfect is not what I might perceive as perfect. Thus, if I help you, I won't do anything right. Perfection is subjective and quite frankly, does not even exist. Attempting to do all of your work and life alone sets you up for failure, not perfectionism. Think of some of the unfulfilled people that you know in life. Many of them are probably unfulfilled because they spent their energies trying to take on roles they didn't even really want to take on or attempted to please people they didn't even care to please. Subsequently, in their attempt to make everything perfect and doing things alone, they isolated themselves. Lack of supports can lead to anxiety, depression and lack of fulfillment.

Sometimes it can be challenging to identify your supports. Earlier we discussed the importance of enjoying your journey. As you become more present in the moment, supports that you did not even know existed at one time might have been there the whole time. For example, your adolescents can be utilized as supports. If you have adolescents, use them! I know what you are saying, and I get that adolescents are takers by nature, but trust me, you can use them to your benefit.

Adolescences have been compared to infants and toddlers. Infants and adolescences both have a lot of physical changes going on. Toddlers have begun to explore their independence and work to discover all the new things they can do alone; crawl, standup, walk, unlock the door that leads to the pool. Yikes. The toddler has limited fear because it has not really experienced the world yet. Similarly, adolescents are exploring their new freedom; they have changing hormones, are trying to fit in, and are "testing the door to the pool." Adolescences have not experienced the real world and the fears and responsibilities it can pose. Just like an infant has to take, take, take to grow, adolescents do, too. However, adolescents can carry heavier weights and that means they can bring up the groceries and take out the trash. Use the fact that your adolescent needs something from you, to your advantage.

What do you want done? Have your adolescent help you, and let them know upfront they will be rewarded for their behavior. Keep your promises, rewards and consequences. You undermine your own authority when you create a punishment or consequence and do not hold to it. Earlier we discussed the importance of your credibility and not taking back your word. This concept is similar with your children. Children can learn how to manipulate and take advantage of you and your authority if you do not hold to what you say you are going to do. When you do not come through on commitments, children will lose respect for you. Just as you must adhere to punishments and consequences you have created for your children, you should come through on promises, too. Coming through on promises increases your child's level of trust in you and also fosters a stronger rapport between you both.

However, it is not your lawful duty to give your adolescent money for recreation, nor should you have guilt for having them help and support you. You have to feed and clothe your children and provide them with shelter. Anything above and beyond should be a reward for the help they provide to you. Ask your children and adolescents for help. Think back to the importance of 50-50 in a relationship. You have a relationship with your child. If your adolescent takes out the trash, makes the bed and starts the laundry; you reward them with money or something that they feel is desirable. While your child is utilizing their reward, instead of taking out the trash and starting the laundry, you can go to that art class you wanted to attend or simply relax and meditate. If you choose to do otherwise, that is your choice. Make the most of your time and use people in a mutually beneficial manner.

Sometimes it is hard to avoid the feelings of guilt associated with asking a child for help. For example, maybe you worked all day and have not seen your child. The last thing you want to do is ask him to complete chores. Mothers possess a lot of guilt when their children are struggling in school, have an absent father or realize that they need more help. The fact is, giving children small tasks and then rewarding them will increase confidence and understanding of real world principles. Having children help you with tasks gets them up and moving as opposed to sitting, where anxiety or depression can brew. Working on household tasks together can build a bond or get a child to open up and talk. In addition, the less housework you have to do, the more activities you can do to work toward fulfillment. The more personal fulfillment you have, the more likely that your responses, interactions and attitudes toward your children will be positive and more valuable. The end result of requesting help is all in the way you reframe each situation and how you deliver the assignments and tasks.

Sometimes women fear that if they ask for help, they will "owe" the other person something in return. The fear of saying "No" to a person, after they have already helped us, stops us from ever even asking for help in the first place. Do not live the same pain twice, especially if the pain might be unnecessary. You are sitting in fear that this person will ask you for something later down the road if they help you out now. You don't even know if they will ask you for help, you just assume that. In fact, you don't even know if they will help you out to begin with. You are willing to suffer without help, just because of the chance that they might need you someday. You might find that they do call on you for assistance in the future, but that the give and take of them helping you and vice versa, actually proves to be beneficial.

Also, you do not always have to help someone out who has helped you in the past. We talked about the importance of having premade answers for the people you are unable to help or that treat you like a doormat. In an event that you can and want to help this person, do so in a way that doesn't turn you into a doormat. Set boundaries with people. Perhaps say "yes" to some part of their request and "No" to other parts. If they want you to pick up their child from school Tuesday, and you will be at the doctor, give them an option that better suits you, but still acknowledges that you want to help. Do things for other people, but do so when it is convenient for you. This might sound like a selfish concept, but the more you can set boundaries in life, the more positive you will feel. The better you feel the more you will give back. You have to give your time and attention to your top five roles before anything else.

There are people that I would not recommend reaching out to for help. If there are people that sabotage you, love to find something wrong with you just to hold it over your head, people that belittle you or people that are manipulators, then do not ask them for help.

The reason is because the benefits do not outweigh the consequences. If more negativity and pain will be caused by asking for help, than in the long run, it is not worth it. It will cost you too many emotions and energy that will not be used on the appropriate life roles. It is easy to call on an old boyfriend to help you when your car breaks down. However, if calling on him will make you feel belittled or abused or you find you will give up your control and confidence to him, remain without a car until you can come up with another solution. There is always another solution. If you can't think of another solution, you are not taking enough time to analyze and reframe the situation. Research shows that people who have depression tend to see things in black and white. The answer is this or that, there is no in between. Black and white thinking limits your brain processing and options. Without options, your control and positive life outlook decrease. Do not think in terms of black and white. There is always an in between. The in between may not be exactly what you want, but there is always another way to look at the same situation and come to a conclusion.

It does take time to create support systems that are healthy. Supportive people may not do everything as you see perfectly, but they genuinely do want to help you work toward feeling fulfilled. Good supports not only take responsibilities off our plates which free up stressors, give us energy and help us work toward fulfillment, but they also bring to awareness our negative behaviors. People don't always see that they are sabotaging themselves. We can be blinded by our perceptions of what we think is moral or right. We are blinded by our own perceptions when it comes to everything. My reality is what I see, and your reality is what you see. Sometimes the consequences of what we do, do not come forward until a later date. For example, sometimes women perceive control over a man as a form of self-protection. If she knows where he is and what he is doing at all times, she can protect herself against the unknown. The fact is, you will never be 100% sure of what anyone is doing all the time. If you channel your energy into trying to control the whereabouts of someone, you will find that your energy is depleted and your anxiety is up. Your partner may not mind this behavior initially, but the more frequently you engage in controlling behaviors, the more likely he is to resent you later on down the road. Resentment leads to conflict in the relationship which could lead to decreased self-confidence or the need for more control.

Good supports are like outsiders who have different perspectives on situations and your behaviors. You might not always agree with a third party, but if this person is not toxic and is perceived as a good support, you should take some of what they are saying into consideration. If you are not aware that you are controlling or that you engage in negative types of behaviors, than how can you ever work through that barrier? If you are unable to identify your barriers, than many of your life goals will not get attained impacting your level of Life fulfillment. You must be self-aware to be self-fulfilled.

What are some issues that supports have brought up to you that you "blew off," that might constitute as a barrier to your success and fulfillment? Do not let your ego or the need to "be right" stop you from answering this question. Be authentic with yourself.

"Funny thing how when you reach out, people tend to reach right back. Best, then, to make sure your hand is open and not fisted."

-Richelle E. Goodrich

Chapter 8

Your Story

Some women are unaware that they have a story. Behind every woman you have this amazing story of a journey that shaped who she is today. The journey might have been a struggle or selfless, but whatever the journey, women tend to minimize their stories or fail to even acknowledge them. As we minimize our story, we fail to give ourselves credit for why we are successful in life and love. The most basic fundamental in upholding our confidence is the consistent reminder that we had and have a journey. Our journey should not be something that happened in the past, we should tell the world about our journey in an appropriate and healthy manner in the present. We should acknowledge our journey every single day. The more we live our journey and experience the in the moment, moments, the more empowered and confident we will feel. The trick is in knowing which story to tell and retell, and how to reframe your story in a manner that shows strength and resilience. The more you tell your story, the more your story shapes you in the present. Make sure the story you are telling shapes the current you, the right way.

Women get this faulty assumption when something good happens to them, that they are "lucky." If we are lucky to have received this job offer, or are lucky to have been married for 40 years, then we have created the potential for fear. We have created fear within ourselves because luck runs out. If you worked hard for something, chances are you earned it and it is not going anywhere, but if you were just lucky, chances are it won't happen again or you are going to lose it. If you acknowledge your story and journey, then when you get promoted or celebrate 40 years of marriage, you see that you created this success over years of hard work, not one quick draw of luck. If you take time to review your story and journey, you will see that there were times you had set backs and maybe even failures, but the point is, you were still successful in the end. Even when you felt like you had moved back, you were moving up. We are all on our journey in life. Some of us have branched off and started new paths, but in the big picture, no matter how many paths you have taken, this is still your one big journey. If you look back at all the paths you have taken and you really do not see any successes, you are looking at everything wrong.

You need to look at your life and reframe the situations you have experienced into something that is more beneficial to the person you are and who you are trying to become. Seeing reality from a stronger perception increases self-confidence and a sense of personal fulfillment. Pretend your journey is a tree in a forest. If you have a negative self-story, go stand on the other side of the tree or look at the tree from a different angle, now retell your story in a positive and empowering light. As you highlight your story, you become both self-aware and less fearful of loss, which may have been one of your barriers. This is your story, you are in charge of the perception that is portrayed to the world and yourself. If you want to look at yourself differently, change some of the wording in your story. Many of us had extremely hard or upsetting pasts, but if we reframe our stories to show our strength, resilience and self-control, the more we tell and retell that story, eventually we become that story. How has the way you have repeatedly told your personal story impacted who you are today?

I will admit, sometimes, I forget my story, too. I recognize that the more I tell my story of strength (or lack thereof) this is who I will become. When my world gets rocky, I self-reflect and acknowledge that this is my body's way of telling me that I am not repeating my story of strength enough. I do get scared that I am going to lose something. Sometimes I do feel that I am lucky to have had an opportunity or lucky to have my family. However, I shouldn't feel guilty saying that I positioned myself appropriately and worked my ass off the opportunities that have come before me. I shouldn't feel guilty that I have worked every day, endlessly, to create the family I have today. When you think about your story in a manner that reflects strength and resilience you increase your confidence. The more we tell our stories, believe in our stories and live our stories, the more our confidence will continue to grow. Our learning is never ending. The more we apply our lessons learned from past experiences into current and future experiences, the more positive we will shape our present and come closer toward self-actualization and fulfillment.

I have lots of stories that created who I am today. I have childhood stories, college stories and motherhood stories. I suppose I could offer you another 20 chapters in this book if I really provided all my stories. I could tell you stories that would make you cry or ponder why I never gave up. Those are pity party stories though. I have to be cognizant of the story I tell to the world. Every story I could tell, whether bad or good has made me who I am. Knowing this, why should I tell my story in a depressing manner? I want to tell my story in a light that reflects my strength and ability to overcome and achieve. I choose to tell my story of success.

I remember writing my dissertation for my doctoral program. I would work all day, then I would come home and my husband would leave for work. Being a newlywed and a new mother, this was really tough emotionally and physically for me and my husband. When my husband would leave for work, he would pass me our new born and all the responsibilities that came with him. I would sit with a pillow over my lap and nurse my son as I typed away the theoretical foundation of my dissertation. My husband and I did not live in close proximity to family, and sometimes I felt really lonely. When my son was two and a half we decided to move three hours south to be closer to family. Logically, I got pregnant again and my husband lost his job. My thought at that time, when it rains it pours, Murphy's Law, unlucky, and every other karma line I could read off. I found myself with my new full time job, my new part time job getting hours for licensure, and taking on a new job as a professor all while enjoying the second and third trimesters of both my pregnancy and dissertation.

Hello! I worked my ass off for my success! Who am I kidding? Why am I self-doubting or minimizing all I have done? I am not lucky. Lucky people aren't being milked like a cow while trying to finish a doctoral program and work three jobs. As I remember my days of being milked, I remember my story and my journey toward success. I am not lucky, and that is a good thing. If life was based solely on luck, we wouldn't be able to control our future and edit our stories. I have a key sitting on my key ring that proves I am in control of my journey.

What is your story? You have one. Even if you have never been milked like a cow and had great parents whose last name was Jones. You have a story and a journey. Some people have stories that we could not fathom; stories of overcoming childhood abuse, cancer, or surviving years of domestic violence. As tough as these stories are, they show the strength of the woman and what she can overcome. It is most challenging to accept our past sometimes, especially the simple yet painful truth that we cannot change it. If you had a traumatic or negative childhood, just remember that you are in control of your second family, where you become wife and mother. We cannot control our first family, but we sure are in control of creating our second one. Let go of grudges, they hurt only you. Only you live with these negative thoughts every day, no one else. Forgive the past and everyone in it, so you can move forward. You do not have to feel forgiveness, you just do it. You deserve freedom.

Regret is painful, especially when we take responsibility and ownership for the situation that took place in which we now regret. Our childhood and situations that led to holding grudges and regret are all unchangeable. What we can change is our perception of the negativity about the events. This is in no way to say you must forget these experiences, remembering them are important to your personal story. Rather, reframe the events into learning experiences which have made you strong enough to help, encourage or protect others. Take your past and reframe it. If you are fully aware that you can't change your past, you are more capable of doing something good with it moving forward. This is because you are not spending all your time and energy trying to prove how bad the past was. People that can't accept what can't be changed, spend so much time dwelling on the situation that they do not have any energy left over to reframe and see how much power they really do have in reshaping their journeys.

If you genuinely accepted your past and never dwelled on it again, how would you be different? How would you make different choices? How would your emotional state be different? If you have a negative story, how has your story of negativity hurt you or others in the past? Remember this, if *you* drink the poison of anger, don't expect the bad guy to die.

Women have such stories of strength, and we must spread this form of success. Women need to empower and encourage other women. I have noticed that women can be really "catty" and hurtful toward other women. I see this a lot in business. I have noticed that some women who get to the top don't push for other women to join them. Perhaps it is an unconscious fear of loss, a fear that she might lose her status by bringing up another woman. Sometimes, women just choose to push others down. It's sad, but that is a reality. Women seem in competition with one another, when we should be rooting for each other. I saw a wonderful quote that said "girls compete with each other, women empower each other." Can you identify one woman that would benefit from your help? Would you be willing to help her? Why or why not? If so, what is something you can do in the near future to help her?

Your story is also not supposed to be told in a manner that shows competition, "my story has more drama than yours." You also do not want to bore people with your endless problems and "I can't get a break" stories. Tell your story so that you and others can see your strength and ability to adapt, change and grow. You may find a sense of fulfillment as you edit your story. Your story is not to be compared to someone else's for a level of intensity. Every woman is unique and has her own story separate of another's. Your story might influence or empower another woman regardless of the intensity and drama it brings. Be authentic when you discuss your story. This is a representation of who you are today and a blueprint of who you are going to become. As you begin to adapt toward a more fulfilled you, you are going to remember your story and what you were passionate about. You also may make changes to your story that requires new habits or elicits new and strong emotions. Today, begin updating your story and pop the balloons left over from last night's pity party.

I will acknowledge that as you tell your story, feelings and emotions will arise, some that are scary or depressing. The challenge is that you must reframe those hurt feelings in a manner that empowers you and demonstrates your strength to overcome, learn and teach. As a woman, you need to be very cautious how you tell your story to others. Sure your mother or best friend will throw you a pity party at times, but the way you tell your story to the rest of the world, could reflect poorly on you. When you tell your story, it is a representation of you in the present. You are creating your reputation and exposing yourself to others who might not be kind. Not only could your story lead to inappropriate gossip from others, but it can ruin your credibility, especially if you are a business owner. Negativity and mental health illnesses are still taboo to some people in society. People might associate your negativity with the type of service they would get if they utilized your business resources. They may also steer clear of you based upon how much support they think they would have to provide you if they took on a role as your partner or friend.

If your story has put you into a negative place, be cautious how you portray your negativity to others. If you are negative, you need positive people in your life to help change your path and ultimately help you create a new story. Guess, what? You know why positive people are positive people? They stay far away from negative people. Negativity truly is contagious. The positive people you need in your life are going to politely decline the invitation to your pity party. Reframe your story into something that shows your ability to overcome, become stronger and teach.

Here is an activity that will assist you in reframing your story. Take out your notebook and write your story as you would normally tell it. Walk away from the story and come back to it at a later date when you are feeling positive and happy. Then, read the story you wrote. How would a happy person view this story? Would they want to be around you? What can you delete from your story, add to your story, or what about strength or self-discovery didn't you mention? Be authentic in your story, but reframe the negativity. You can acknowledge the negativity, but dwelling on it and creating and entire story based on how bad things were is not appropriate or effective. The more you tell your story in a negative manner, the more you personally reinforce the negativity in your life. Conversely, the more you tell your story in a positive manner, the more you personally reinforce the positivity in your life. Create a habit of telling a story of strength and you will become this story.

How can your journey be turned into a story of powerfulness, strength and resilience? What have you learned from your new story? To whom can you share your new story with?

"You must have control of the authorship of your own destiny. The pen that writes your life story must be held in your own hand." - Irene Kassorla

Chapter 9

Type "S"uperwoman

Superwoman, your time has come. Prepare your cape for takeoff. What has the past eight chapters taught you? We have learned to tell our own story, reach out to supports, define our goals and track our successes. We have learned to be more comfortable, define our barriers and be more confident. We have also chosen our top five life roles and reflected on their importance. We are finally going to stop the Ferris Wheel. We are stepping off. We are giving up the juggling act that we do so well, taking off the different hats we wear, and putting on one single cape. The time has come to achieve balance between Life and Work. As a true SuperWoman you now know that there is a strong importance in setting aside time for your own personal wellness and health.

When I first began leading up the SuperWoman workshops, I began the journey in Tampa, Florida. I was asked to write for a motherhood blog site. The first question talked about Super Women in general and how a workshop like mine could put pressure on women because of how many responsibilities they already have. The question asked was put in a manner that appeared I was encouraging women how to be Super Women (two words). They were right; hosting a seminar like that would put pressure on women. The good news for me was that this seminar was the exact opposite of what they thought.

That evening I knew that this workshop was going to help women all over the country find fulfillment. I am not teaching you how to become a Super Woman, you are already a pro at that. I am teaching you how to become a SuperWoman (one word). In order to be a real SuperWoman, you have to achieve balance. We are all Super Women, and juggle 50-60 things at a time and go well beyond serving our top five life roles. However, to be a real SuperWoman, you must achieve balance between Life and Work. You ride the Ferris Wheel, but not all day every day. You step off and enjoy moments. You are fulfilled and confident.

In this book we have addressed barriers to our goals and ultimate fulfillment. You have analyzed how these barriers decrease productivity and encourage less authenticity. Barriers stop us from moving forward, make us feel guilty, or riddle us with anger. The ability to possess self-control isn't always easy, but the more control you have the more you will be in tune with your body and mind. You have the freedom to control your present, future and overall fulfillment. Understanding and truly believing in this concept are the early creations of a SuperWoman.

A real SuperWoman admits her faults and is willing to take responsibility for what is happening around her. Everything that happens to you is based upon your perception and your personal reality. Life is subjective to all people. Work-Life balance for me is different from Work-Life balance for you. The way I feel I should be treated in a relationship is different from the way you think you should be treated. What I constitute as success might not constitute as success for you. Life and all its happenings are subjective to each person. A SuperWoman accepts the fact that people perceive experiences differently than she does, and she respects that. This is why she does not strive for perfectionism, rather self-actualization.

As tough as it may be, a SuperWoman takes responsibility for her emotions. Her pain, lack of fulfillment and anxiety is based upon her perception of the world and interactions she has. If she has the power to create her own pain, she has the super powers to create her own happiness. Life is completely unfair at times. That's a statement. There are no "buts" or "whys." That's it. Life is unfair. Now what? Deal with it. A SuperWoman accepts that life is unfair and when she isn't holding the best cards in her hand, she still wins the round because her positive attitude trumped everyone. A positive attitude wins every time because it keeps you open minded to finding alternate solutions to winning and success.

Think about a time in your life when things were really tough for you. You picked up your cards and they were different suits and you had no matches. Every time you drew a new card, a worse one fell into your hand. You were irritated and almost felt defeated at the first round. How could you have played this hand of life differently? The answer is definitely not, "There was nothing I could have done differently." Think about how you could have altered your attitude, associated with different people or made different choices. The next time you are faced with a whole hand of cards in different suits and you have no clue what you are going to do, stop, put on your cape, and complete the activities from this book again.

SuperWomen take time to assess the people in their lives and rid of the toxic people. Toxic people are people in your life that suck you emotionally dry, stir anger within you or treat you like a doormat. Sometimes toxic people are fun and exciting. The fun and exciting ones can possess the most toxicity. This is usually the ex-boyfriend, the bad boy or the female "best friend" that sucks you emotionally and mentally dry. She is also the one who has time to gossip to you and about you. This is the friend that you talk to over the phone, and when you hang up, you feel worse than you did when you initially called her. Rid of her. It does not matter that you have known her since kindergarten. She is deleting your hard earned energy dollars.

I advise women that are hooked on toxic partners to create a fantasy breaker. You are to list out all the things you do not like about this toxic person, and look at it every time you have doubts about not being with them. Break the fantasy that your mind creates to trick you into taking this person back. False fantasies are barriers in disguise. Put the fantasy breaker list in your phone and read it at least once a day. Your toxic partner will not be different this time around. Do not out smart your common sense. You broke up for a reason. Do not decide to go back with someone who hurt you when you are in an emotional state. This means you can't give into hooks. Manipulative people are good at knowing what you love and feeding you that in order to "hook" you or regain control. The more in control you are, the better plan you have, the more manipulators will give you everything you ever wanted. Bite the hook though, and you're caught.

As a future SuperWoman, I ask that you pull out your journal or a notebook, and write down all the people that are toxic in your life. The bi-polars (these people take you up and down. I love you, I hate you), the criers, the takers, the down-right mean people, the users, the bull-shitters, the gossipers, the passive aggressives. Circle the ones you know you can get rid of first and erase them like you hit the delete button on your computer. I understand that there are people that you can't or may not want to rid of that are toxic. Mothers and fathers can sometimes be toxic and very hurtful. With people that are toxic that you choose not to rid of, you must set clear boundaries with them.

Some people say you are what you eat. I say, you are who you associate with. People are typically a combination of the top three to five people they associate with most. Take a moment to reflect on the people you spend most of your time with. What characteristics do you share with them, positive or negative?

The toxic people that still remain in your life, what attachment do you have with them? Why don't you want to rid of them? Is there a way you can set boundaries with these people or wean off of them? If so, how?

List of Toxic People in my Life

1._____

2._____

3._____

4._____

5._____

*For a printable version go to: www.typesuperwoman.com and click on the link that says, "SuperWoman Worksheets."

As hard as it is to accept responsibility, a SuperWoman knows that if she plans to keep toxic people in her life, and then one of them hurts her, ultimately, she let them. This is your choice. You know their patterns, you labeled them toxic, but yet you kept them around your happiness and are willing to spend your energy dollars on them. As the toxic people fade away, you have more time for you, your fulfillment and your top five life roles; these are traits of a SuperWoman.

What is a Type S personality? Let's begin here. Are you Type A or Type B personality? A Type A personality is described as proactive, overly organized, cares for others, a super achiever who takes on way too much, and hates being late or people around them being late. Type B personalities on the other hand, consist of people who want to achieve, but are not extremely upset when they do not. They are steady in their work and laid back on several issues. Type B's do enjoy the moment.

I will admit, when choosing between a Type A and Type B personality, I am a Type A. Although it is great to be successful and achieve (which both Type A's and B's do), the stress and torment that comes from the pressure I put on myself, sometimes unnecessarily, is really bad for my physical and mental health. Some studies show that Type A personalities have double the chance of having a heart attack when compared to Type B's. I am going to obtain all this success and achieve all my dreams and then kick the can?! This cannot be good. I think of a Type A personality when I hear the quote, "A man spends his life getting his wealth, and then spends all his wealth on getting back his health."

Some Type A personalities live life at a stress level of seven to nine day in and day out, whereas Type B's live at much lower stress levels. Living at such high stress levels is not good for your overall health. Living at a stress level of nine is like living your life in crisis mode. We discussed how living in crisis mode is a real danger to your body emotionally and physically and also impacts your decision making. When you live in fight or flight mode all the time, when a problem does come your way, you will find that you have depleted all your energy.

If you were going to run a 5K, and before the 5K you ran for eight hours straight, when the time came to run the 5K, you would be out of breath. Why the heck did you run for eight hours straight before the race even began? That was not necessary. When you run yourself to the ground trying to be perfect and trying to overachieve on every little thing in life, when you are really needed up for bat, you do not perform. This is where we end up having mental break downs, panic attacks and even suicide attempts. The body gets to a point where it cannot face exalting another moment of energy, let alone now going up for a real battle. The body protects itself and sometimes it thinks that the best protection is to shut down. The problem is, whether you are down or not, your husband, children, job and everything else on your list of duties, needs you. You can't be down. This is why a Super Woman is different from a SuperWoman. A real SuperWoman is well aware that no matter how hard she strives, she will never be perfect, and this is okay.

There are two forms of perfectionism, adaptive and maladaptive. SuperWomen are adaptive perfectionists. This type of perfectionism is very similar to those who are consistently striving toward self-actualization. An adaptive perfectionist strives for a certain high standard, but is not solely fixated on reaching the goal. She enjoys the journey. If she does not reach her goal, she does not become overly critical of herself. The event is processed as a lesson learned and she moves forward. She adds this event as part of her story and tells it in a manner that conveys her level of strength and resilience. You can take any experience, from any single person, and we each will see it differently. We also can take any story and tell it differently. Your story can be read multiple ways. Let's think back to the tree in the forest. You stand in front of the tree and I will walk behind it. We must each talk about the tree. Your story will be quite different from mine because of the perception that we are both getting from the same tree. Perfection is subjective, thus perfection is but reality to only one person. Perfect to me is different from perfect to you. John Dewey said, "Not perfection as a final goal, but the ever enduring process of perfecting, maturing, refining is the aim of living." A Superwoman strives for goals not perfectionism.

Here's the shocker, you don't want to live your life as a Type A or a Type B person. You want to be a strong, Type S. Type SuperWoman. Type S is workaholic meets Fijian Islands. Imagine being placed with your work laptop on a raft near the shore of Fiji. Carlos the Cabana Boy is bringing you red drinks with little umbrellas and the wind is whisking your raft slowly down the shore. You have to stop and take in the moment. You are forced to. You do a little work, you kick a little sand, and then you do it again. Until the drinks set in, at which time you get some much needed rest. While I am fully aware we cannot all relocate to Fiji, I do believe that we can find this balance of a little work, a little sand.

Welcome to the island of Type S personality. Type S seems like it could be easy to achieve, (who doesn't like Carlos the Cabana boy?). Actually, achieving a strong Type S personality is harder than one might think, especially because we are creatures of habit and easily succumb to guilt. We talked earlier about being creatures of habit. People are who they are. It is quite challenging to change. If you have brushed than flossed your teeth, in that order, for 40 years, it would be hard to suddenly change that order up and floss than brush. Even if you did change the order, after a couple weeks, you would probably revert back out of habit. As you begin to work toward developing your Type S personality, you will discover that it is really easy to let the trials of life or the quick pace of our lifestyle shove you back into a Type A or Type B personality, and back on to the Ferris Wheel. Changing and self-improving becomes a full time life role. You must be present with yourself, choices, decisions, and actions, every minute of the day. That takes work.

A SuperWoman lists out her top five life roles, and she is one of those life roles. When I lead up the SuperWoman workshops, I have yet to find a woman that puts her own name on the top five life roles. When I ask the women, "Did you make the list?," the women often reply, "Oh, I am supposed to be on here, too?" By the end of each seminar, all the women have restructured their life roles lists to include themselves. They are no longer guilty being on their own list and finding fulfillment. It is my hope, that after writing this book, more and more women put their own names on their top five life roles lists.

During the SuperWomen workshops, women transform scrapbooks into vision books. I encourage them to work quickly and efficiently. I allow one full hour during the workshop to create these vision books. I allot this amount of time because we are creatures of habit and lack giving ourselves personal time. Chances are, not all the women will leave this seminar and actually complete their vision books. The workshop is guaranteed personal time to work on this task.

During my Tampa workshop, I encouraged the women to complete their vision books at some point in the near future if they did not complete them during the seminar. I encouraged the women to open their planners and schedule a time within the next week for only them. This time was not to be overridden by anything and must be treated as if it were a business meeting they could not cancel. Ten minutes into scrapbooking, one of the ladies who owned a fitness studio stated that she needed to leave but that she promised she would complete her vision book. That night I had realized I forgot to give her the SuperWoman Certificate of completion. Later that week I was scheduled to work out at her facility. I emailed her the day of and advised her that I would be working out at 5:30 and I would bring along her SuperWoman Certificate. The woman advised me that she would not be there and to leave the SuperWoman Certificate on her desk. She informed me that 5:30 on this particular day was the day that she had scheduled her personal time with herself and was unable to break the appointment! It was then that I knew she deserved that certificate. I placed the certificate on the SuperWoman's desk proudly.

That same evening, I got a Facebook picture of her completed scrapbook turned into a vision book. I was beyond thrilled for her. However, I must be confident enough to give myself credit as well. I have a personal story. Not all of my stories are pretty. Many of my stories do not end "happily ever after." But the story I live by and tell has helped me to achieve things that allow me to pass on my motivation and knowledge to others. I may not have played a huge role in who this woman is today, but I did play a role in this specific experience in her life, and it was empowering, for us both. A real SuperWoman shares her story of strength, lessons learned, and positively influences people with it.

As you strengthen yourself, you create more energy to tackle other, less important "have to's" in life. You may also find that you can bank some extra energy dollars to rebound easily from set- backs. A real SuperWoman does not live in crisis mode. She banks her energy dollars for major decisions and critical issues that could arise. When major decisions arise, a real SuperWoman is confident in her actions and thoughts. Her decisions are not based solely on emotion and are not impulsive. SuperWomen know the negativity associated with making decisions at low points. Proper and confident decision making immediately aligns us with our next opportunity or decision. Chances are, if we make a strong and healthy decision, we will be aligned with positive opportunities and the potential for further fulfillment.

Below is a list of characteristics of a SuperWoman. I encourage you to print out a copy and keep it somewhere visible so you are consistently reminded to work toward personal fulfillment and self-actualization. I suggest you select two or three characteristics off of this list, highlight them and begin to work toward enhancing this aspect of yourself. Here are the characteristics that compose a Type "S"uperWoman's personality:

CHARACTERISTICS OF A SUPERWOMAN

1. A SuperWoman is authentic with herself.
2. A SuperWoman has identified her top five life roles.
3. A SuperWoman focuses on giving 100% to her top five roles.
4. A SuperWoman understands that she can do anything she wants, but she can't do everything.
5. A SuperWoman understands the differences between "kindness" and "doormat."
6. A SuperWoman is not guilty saying NO to people that have mistaken her for a doormat.
7. A SuperWoman sets boundaries with people who are negative that she cannot rid of.
8. A SuperWoman sets boundaries with all people, even spouses, children and co-workers.
9. A SuperWoman is aware and can catch her own negative or self-sabotaging thoughts.
10. A SuperWoman is able to reframe her own negative thoughts.
11. A SuperWoman is aware and understands what barriers she frequently encounters.
12. A SuperWoman has a plan to work through her barriers.
13. A SuperWoman controls her actions and reactions.

14. A SuperWoman accepts the fact that she can't change the past, but that she is control of her future. This goes for her childhood, grudges and regret.

15. A SuperWoman is aware that she cannot control others, she can guide them, but she can't drive their car for them.

16. A SuperWoman can separate or compartmentalize her frustrations.

17. A SuperWoman does not hold someone at fault for long because she knows she is only hurting herself at that point.

18. A SuperWoman admits when she is wrong.

19. A SuperWoman works toward fulfilling HER bucket list.

20. A SuperWoman can be simple and enjoy the moment.

21. A SuperWoman rewards herself every day. Little successes and being helpful toward others deserve a reward every time.

22. A SuperWoman acknowledges that she is not "lucky," she has earned her status.

23. A SuperWoman does not make decisions at low or angry points.

24. A SuperWoman has healthy support systems.

25. A SuperWoman rids of her toxic "friends."

26. A SuperWoman stays away from negative people.

27. A SuperWoman asks for help when she is ill.

28. A SuperWoman asks for help when she is not ill.

29. A SuperWoman has identified and embraces her story.

30. A SuperWoman doesn't ask people to bring balloons to her pity party.

31. A SuperWoman tells her story in a manner that reflects strength and resilience.

32. A SuperWoman uses the negativity from her past to help others by giving, supporting or teaching them.

33. A SuperWoman consciously focuses on recreating new and healthier habits.

34. A SuperWoman is not Type A or Type B, she is Type S.

35. _____

36. _____

37. _____

38. _____

39. _____

40. _____

*For a printable version go to: www.typesuperwoman.com and click on the link that says, "SuperWoman Worksheets."

These characteristics define a Superwoman. However, after self-searching and reformulating your goals, you may have identified additional traits that you feel constitute as characteristics of a SuperWoman. Feel free to add the SuperWoman characteristics you come up with to the list above or go to www.superwomanblog.net and add some of the characteristics that you feel define a real SuperWoman.

"The secret of change is to focus all of your energy, not on fighting the old, but on building the new." –Socrates

SuperWoman, you are ready to take flight!

Once you have participated in the activities in this book and done so authentically, you can sign your SuperWoman certificate on the following page. *For a printable version go to: www.typesuperwoman.com and click on the link that says, "SuperWoman Worksheets."

Official SuperWoman

This certificate hereby confers upon

_____

The license of

SuperWoman

Specialization in Work-Life Balance

Made in the USA
San Bernardino, CA
04 January 2014